EASTER, PASSOVER,
AND OTHER
SPRING FESTIVALS

HOLIDAYS AND CELEBRATIONS

Carnival
Christmas and Hanukkah
Easter, Passover, and Other Spring Festivals
Halloween and Commemorations of the Dead
Independence Days
Lent, Yom Kippur, and Other Atonement Days
Ramadan
Religious New Year's Celebrations
Thanksgiving and Other Harvest Festivals
Western and Chinese New Year's Celebrations

EASTER, PASSOVER,
AND OTHER
SPRING FESTIVALS

Ann
Morrill

CHELSEA HOUSE
PUBLISHERS
An imprint of Infobase Publishing

Easter, Passover, and Other Spring Festivals

Copyright © 2009 by Infobase Publishing

Chelsea House
An imprint of Infobase Publishing
132 West 31st Street
New York NY 10001

Library of Congress Cataloging-in-Publication Data

Morrill, Ann.
Easter, Passover, and other spring festivals/Ann Morrill.
    p. cm.—(Holidays and celebrations)
Includes bibliographical references and index.
ISBN 978-1-60413-099-7
1. Fasts and feasts—Juvenile literature. 2. Spring festivals—Juvenile literature.
I. Title. II. Series.
BL590.M67 2009
394.265—dc22

                                    2009006915

Chelsea House books are available at special discounts when purchased in bulk quantities for businesses, associations, institutions, or sales promotions. Please call our Special Sales Department in New York at (212) 967-8800 or (800) 322-8755.

You can find Chelsea House on the World Wide Web at
http://www.chelseahouse.com

Produced by Print Matters, Inc.
Text design by A Good Thing, Inc.
Cover design by Alicia Post

Printed in China

CP PMI 10 9 8 7 6 5 4 3 2 1

This book is printed on acid-free paper.

All links and Web addresses were checked and verified to be correct at the time of publication. Because of the dynamic nature of the Web, some addresses and links may have changed since publication and may no longer be valid.

Contents

ि

Introduction to Holidays and Celebrations.................................. vi

INTRODUCTION
Easter 3
Passover 11
Navruz... 19
Holi 25

REGIONAL TRADITIONS AND CUSTOMS
Africa.. 32
Asia... 41
Europe... 52
Latin America and the Caribbean 65
Middle East 75
North America 80
Oceania 98

Glossary 101
Bibliography 104
Further Resources... 105
Picture Credits 107
Index 108
About the Author... 111

Introduction to Holidays and Celebrations

Holidays mark time. They occupy a space outside of ordinary events and give shape and meaning to our everyday existence. They also remind us of the passage of time as we reflect on Christmases, Passovers, or Ramadans past. Throughout human history, nations and peoples have marked their calendars with special days to celebrate, commemorate, and memorialize. We set aside times to reflect on the past and future, to rest and renew physically and spiritually, and to simply have fun.

In English we call these extraordinary moments "holidays," a contraction of the term "holy day." Sometimes holidays are truly holy days—the Sabbath, Easter, or Eid al-Fitr, for example—but they can also be nonreligious occasions that serve political purposes, address the social needs of communities and individuals, or focus on regional customs and games.

This series explores the meanings and celebrations of holidays across religions and cultures around the world. It groups the holidays into volumes according to theme (such as *Lent, Yom Kippur, and Other Atonement Days; Thanksgiving and Other Harvest Festivals; Independence Days; Easter, Passover, and Other Spring Festivals; Western and Chinese New Year's Celebrations; Religious New Year's Celebrations; Carnival; Ramadan*; and *Halloween and Commemorations of the Dead*) or by their common human experience due to their closeness on the calendar (such as *Christmas and Hanukkah*). Each volume is divided into two sections—the first introduces readers to the origins, history, and common practices associated with the holidays; and the second section takes the reader on a worldwide tour that shows the regional variations and distinctive celebrations within specific countries. The reader will learn how these holidays started, what they mean to the people who celebrate them, and how different cultures celebrate them.

These volumes have an international focus, and thus readers will be able to learn about diversity both at home and throughout the world. We can learn a great deal about a people or nation by the holidays they celebrate. We can also learn from holidays how cultures and religions have interacted and mingled over time. We see in celebrations not just the past through tradition, but the principles and traits that people embrace and value today.

The Chelsea House Holidays and Celebrations series surveys this rich and varied festive terrain. Its 10 volumes show the distinct ways that people all over the world infuse ordinary life with meaning, purpose, or joy. The series cannot be all-inclusive or the last word on so vast a subject, but it offers a vital first step for those eager to learn more about the diverse, fascinating, and vibrant cultures of the world, through the festivity that gives expression, order, and meaning to their lives.

Christians hold an Easter vigil celebrating the Resurrection of Jesus Christ in Caracas, Venezuela.

Introduction

⊙ ⊙ ⊙

Since early human beings first walked the Earth, spring has been a time to celebrate the renewal of the land, the source of nourishment for a community. Before agriculture, hunter-gatherer societies practiced rituals centered on the spring equinox. The spring equinox is the time in the spring when the Sun crosses the equator, and the length of the day and the night are equal. For many thousands of years of human history, in temperate climates, surviving the early spring meant survival for the year. Early spring rituals were timed with big hunts, and later with important plantings and other farming events. Ancient people could not jump into their minivans and drive to the grocery store. Their survival depended on growing food. They held rites and rituals to welcome the warmer weather and keep the corn, yam, and wheat spirits pleased. People feared that if these deities were not happy, the Sun would not shine, or there would be too much rain or, worse, there would be no rain and then plants would not grow. The ancient celebrations of spring, while often merry, were also a matter of life and death to a community. The modern springtime celebrations draw some of this ancient energy. Spring festivals sometimes overlap with New Year's celebrations as many ancient civilizations began their new year in spring, when they planted crops for the forthcoming year.

While today thousands of spring celebrations are enjoyed around the globe in the form of neo-pagan rites and environmental occasions such as Earth Day and Arbor Day, four festivals are widely observed by many cultures living in many places—from Liechtenstein to India, Argentina to Zanzibar, and everywhere in between. These four are the Hindu celebration of Holi that originated in southern Asia, the Persian new year festival Navruz, the Jewish observance of Passover (or "Pesach" in Hebrew), and the Christian Easter celebration.

Although each celebration has distinct rites and traditions, all of them share a common purpose with the ancient spring rites: They honor life and rebirth and the triumph of good over evil. As each holiday is observed, the faithful are encouraged to reflect on their actions and behavior and how they affect loved ones. At each celebration families and communities gather, dressed in holiday costumes or new clothes, to enjoy special foods and exchange small gifts. For Jews and Persians, the spring festival is also a time to clean the home and rid it of unwanted items.

Easter

Easter is considered the most important Christian festival. Easter celebrates the central Christian belief that Jesus rose from dead three days after his Crucifixion. Christians believe Jesus was the Son of God, and died on the cross to redeem humanity from sin. In addition to its religious meaning, the Resurrection symbolizes the revival of hope and a fresh lease on life for all human beings. Christ's victory over death signifies to Christians the possible salvation of their eternal souls.

Origins of Easter

Eostre, the Mother Goddess

The English name for this celebration, *Easter*, takes its name from the pagan deity Eostre, the mother goddess of the Saxon tribes of northern

A saleswoman polishes Easter bunnies on display for sale in Düsseldorf, Germany. The Easter egg–delivering bunnies are a typical Easter symbol.

Europe. Eostre was also the goddess of fertility. She was believed to be in charge of conception and birth, as well as pollination, flowering, and the ripening of fruit. After the harsh dreary winters of northern Europe, Eostre brought the warmth of spring, fertility, and abundance.

The ancient deities in all civilizations had patron animals, and the rabbit, a symbol of fertility, is the companion animal of Eostre. In one legend, Eostre transformed a bird into a rabbit—but the rabbit kept the ability to lay eggs. Eostre's feast day occurred on the first full Moon following the spring equinox. Celebrants would combine prayers of thanks and make small offerings over fires.

Rebirth in the Mediterranean

Most of the pagan societies that settled in the Mediterranean region had a major religious celebration at or following shortly after the spring equinox. A common theme of these spring religious festivals was a god whose own death and rebirth symbolized the death and regeneration of life during this time of year. There are stories of a few gods in pagan religions who were believed to have died only to be reborn.

For example, the Phrygian fertility goddess, Cybele, had a consort named Attis. (Phrygia was located within the triangle formed by the modern cities of Afyon, Eskisehir, and Ankara, the capital of modern Turkey.) Attis was believed to have been born of a virgin, and several religious historians believe that the Christian legends of death and resurrection were first associated with him. The ancient Christians, on the other hand, claimed that Satan had created counterfeit, or false, deities to preempt the debut of Jesus and to confuse humanity. Modern-day Christians, those who know of it, regard the Attis legend as merely a pagan myth. They believe the account of Jesus' death and Resurrection and do not accept the idea that it might be related to the earlier tradition.

The Arrival of Christianity

With the arrival of Christianity, sweeping changes took place in these ancient spring rites and ceremonies, first within cultures located along the Mediterranean and later through the lands of Europe. In order to promote Christianity as the only religion, early church leaders banned all pagan rites and ceremonies. But these rituals had been a way of life for thousands of years, and people did not easily give them up. So the Christian Church adapted, attaching Christian meanings to the old pagan rituals and festivals.

One Last Blowout

For many parts of Europe and the Americas, Easter season begins with a celebration called Carnival or Mardi Gras that generally features carousing, eating, and drinking, and masked processions through cities and towns. Carnival celebrations take place in many countries around the world, especially those with large Roman Catholic populations, such as much of Latin America and the Caribbean, and areas where historically the French had power, such as New Orleans, Louisiana, and Montreal, Canada. The festivities end on Shrove Tuesday, the day before Ash Wednesday, which is the first day of Lent.

Christian Easter

The Crucifixion of Jesus took place on what is now called Good Friday. In the early morning of the third day after his Crucifixion, which happened to be Sunday, some women disciples of Jesus went to the cave (tomb) where his body had been laid. They learned that Jesus had been resurrected, or raised from the tomb. Grief turned into celebration following this amazing occurrence.

Easter is not a festival confined to a single day, however. It is spread over a considerable length of time, starting with Lent, a period of spiritual preparation for Easter. In some countries, those in which Roman Catholicism is the dominant religion in particular, Easter celebrations begin with Carnival. Carnival is called Mardi Gras ("Fat Tuesday") in French-speaking countries.

When Easter Is Celebrated

Easter is called a "movable feast," because it is celebrated on different dates every year. The Western and Eastern

Easter and the Moon

Even today, nature guides church planning. Christians celebrate Easter on the first Sunday after the first full Moon of spring.

Holiday Schedules

The date of the Christian celebration of Easter is linked to the ancient Jewish celebration of Pesach or Passover. The Jewish people followed the Persian (Babylonian) calendar and their new year commenced with the spring equinox.

Churches celebrate Easter at different times because they use different methods to schedule the holiday.

Roman Catholic and Protestant Churches of the West schedule Easter using a complicated system of rules that date to the Council of Nicea. At that meeting in 325, church leaders came up with a number of rules about how the Roman Catholic Church should work. One thing they decided was that the Church should hold a holiday to commemorate the day on which Jesus rose from the dead. Because they didn't know when this happened, they decided that Easter would be celebrated on the Sunday after the first full Moon following the spring equinox. Helpful astronomers created a chart that plotted out their estimates of the dates of full Moons for many years to come. The Church formally adopted these dates as what are called "ecclesiastical full Moons." They noted that the spring equinox fell on March 20 in 325, so they made that an official date. From then on, the rule for scheduling Easter was that Easter should fall on the first Sunday after the first ecclesiastical full Moon after March 20. The result of this complicated scheduling is that the Western Easter can fall anywhere between March 22 and April 25.

The Eastern Orthodox Easter usually comes after the Western Easter. There are several reasons for this. First, the Eastern Churches do not use the same calendar as the Western Churches. Western Churches use the Gregorian calendar, which is the calendar that is used in Canada, Europe, the United States, and most of the world. The Eastern Churches use the Julian calendar, which was the calendar in place when the rules for scheduling Easter were first set. The Julian calendar is currently 13 days ahead of the Gregorian calendar. Second, Eastern Churches use the actual first full Moon after the spring equinox to set the date of Easter. They do not use the ecclesiastical full Moons. Third, the Orthodox Easter must fall after the Jewish holiday of Passover. This is to remain faithful to the Bible's claim that Jesus died after Passover. With these regulations, April 3 is the

A Russian woman lights a candle to celebrate Easter at a church in Moscow. Eastern Orthodox churches, which observe the ancient Julian calendar, usually celebrate Easter later than Western Churches.

earliest date on which the Eastern Churches can celebrate Easter. Sometimes the Eastern Orthodox Easter falls on the same date as it does for Western Churches. In other years it might be as many as five weeks later.

The 40 Days of Lent

Lent is the period before Easter that some Christian churches observe as a time of prayer, fasting, and abstinence. Abstinence means giving up a pleasure (such as chocolate). Lent commences on Ash Wednesday and concludes on Holy Saturday, the day before Easter Sunday. Originally, various Christian groups established the observance as an interval ranging from a few days to several weeks. Eventually it was fixed in the eighth century at 40 days, representing the 40 days that Jesus spent fasting in the wilderness. Among Roman Catholics, Lent lasts for six-and-a-half weeks before Easter, excluding Sundays. According to

Easter Cycles

The cycle of Easter dates repeats itself every 84 years in the Western Churches and every 19 years in the Eastern Churches. In other words, Easter this year will fall on the same date as it did 84 years ago and will fall 84 years from now in the Western Churches. In the Eastern Churches it will fall on the same date as it did 19 years ago and will fall 19 years from now.

Wash Feet and Show Love

Maundy Thursday commemorates the Last Supper, the final meal Jesus shared with his 12 apostles. Maundy Thursday takes its name from the French *mandé*, which comes from the Latin *mandatum*, and means *command*. At the Last Supper, Jesus washed his apostles' feet, commanding them, "Love one another as I have loved you." The foot-washing tradition is still carried out in many Catholic and Protestant Churches around the world today. This day reminds all Christians of the need to love their fellow human beings and all living creatures.

the Eastern Orthodox Churches, it comprises a full eight weeks since Saturdays and Sundays are both excluded.

The last Sunday before Easter (and the first day of Holy Week) is Palm Sunday. This day commemorates the day that Jesus and his disciples entered the city of Jerusalem, where people were gathering for the Jewish festival of Passover. When Jesus arrived there was great excitement among those who believed that he was the long-awaited king of the Jews. People welcomed him by waving palm fronds and spreading palm branches as a carpet across his path.

The most somber of Christian holidays, Good Friday observes the day on which Jesus was crucified by the Romans, who were threatened by his growing influence and power. As the story is told in the Gospels, the biblical accounts of Jesus' life, Jesus was arrested by Roman soldiers in the garden of Gethsemane after being betrayed by one of his disciples, Judas Iscariot. The Romans marched Jesus through the streets and presented

Seder and the Lamb of God

The Crucifixion of Jesus occurred at the same time that the paschal lambs (for the Jewish feast of Passover) were being slaughtered. Jesus came to symbolize the sacrificed lamb of God.

him to the Roman governor Pontius Pilate, who sentenced him to death. The soldiers then put a crown of thorns on Jesus' head and paraded him to the crucifixion site outside of the city. While his disciples watched, the Romans nailed Jesus to the cross, and he died. Later, Jesus' disciples took his body down from the cross and buried him in a tomb, which they closed with a heavy rock.

The Resurrection

Easter is a joyous time in the Christian faith because Jesus' story does not end with his death. Early Sunday morning, Mary Magdalene and several other disciples went to his tomb and were astonished to find that the rock had been moved and the body had vanished. Two angels appeared before the women and explained that Jesus had risen from the dead. Jesus later appeared before the disciples, telling them to spread his teachings throughout the world. Belief in the Resurrection is central to the Christian faith, and Easter is the holiest of Christian holidays.

Celebrating Easter

Easter is celebrated by Protestants, Catholics, and Orthodox Christians throughout the world, especially in Europe, the Americas, and parts

Children prepare to present flowers to the ladies of the church during an Easter children's service at a church in Daytona Beach, Florida.

The Origin of Easter Baskets

Easter baskets originated with the Catholic custom of taking the food prepared for Easter dinner to Mass to be blessed. This custom may have evolved from the ancient ritual of bringing the first crops and seedlings to the temple to ensure a good growing season.

of Africa and Oceania. Most Christians attend church services Easter Sunday morning. They often enjoy a special meal with family and friends after church. On Easter morning in Europe and much of North America, children receive Easter baskets full of candy and sometimes small toys. These baskets are said to have been left by a magical figure called the Easter Bunny. The bunny also hides colored eggs for children to find. In the Western world, many non-Christians participate in Easter festivities related to the bunny rather than the church. It is believed that the hare became part of the Easter tradition first in Germany more than two centuries ago, when parents delighted children with stories about a hare that could lay eggs. The legend is connected with Eostre, who is called *Oastara* in German; the German word for Easter is "Osteon."

Passover

Passover commemorates the departure of the early Jews, or Hebrews, from Egypt and the origin of a Jewish state led by Moses about 3,000 years ago. Passover signifies both the physical as well as the spiritual freedom earned by the Jews. The tale of the Jews' mass exodus is told in the book of Exodus in the Tanakh, or Hebrew Bible (which also forms the largest part of the Christian Bible, the old Testament). Though it is mainly celebrated to remember the Exodus of the Jews from Egypt after centuries of slavery, the festival also marks the beginning of the harvest season in Israel.

The Origin of Passover

The Story of Jacob

According to the book of Exodus, Jacob, with his 70 family members, traveled to Egypt to live a better life and escape a massive famine in Canaan (today's Palestine). Jacob's son Joseph also lived in Egypt, where he had won the favor of the pharaoh of Egypt with his wisdom and had been appointed the viceroy to govern the kingdom. Over the next 430 years the Hebrews prospered in Egypt, and their strength increased to 3 million. Their growing numbers and power became a cause of worry for the pharaoh, who thought that the Hebrews might side with his enemies to dethrone him. So he commanded that the Hebrews work as slaves, engaged in building roads and cities for him. He thought that this hardship would make the Hebrews so exhausted at the end of the day that they would have no time or energy to beget children. The Israelites were also confined to an area known as Goshen (the fertile land lying east of the Nile Delta and west of the Palestinian border).

When even this step did not help to slow the population growth of the Israelites, the pharaoh ordered that all Israeli male babies be killed at birth. However, the Hebrew midwives Shifra and Puah, who were appointed by the pharaoh to kill the male babies, feared the wrath of God and did not follow the pharaoh's orders.

The Story of Moses

Moses, who would become the leader of the Hebrews, was born around the time of the pharaoh's decree that all Israeli male babies be killed at birth was issued. To save her son from being murdered, Moses' mother, Jochebed, placed her child in a basket in the Nile as Moses' sister Miriam watched from a distance to see who would spot the child. The infant was ultimately found by the pharaoh's daughter. She named the child *Moses*, which means "drawn out," as he was literally drawn out of the river, and also unknowingly appointed Jochebed as his nurse. Thus, Moses' real mother was able to make certain he knew his Hebrew heritage.

Moses lived in Midian, an area situated in present-day Saudi Arabia along the eastern shores of the Red Sea, as a shepherd. One day Moses had a vision from God (referred to as the incident of the burning bush), who told him that he and his brother Aaron were the chosen ones to lead the Hebrews out of Egypt into the Promised Land, Canaan. Hesitating initially, Moses and Aaron eventually returned to Egypt.

Finally, Moses, under the guidance of God, led his people out of Egypt after God had sent a series of 10 plagues. These plagues had been meant to warn the pharaoh that if he did not let the Hebrews go then

Two students, left and right, play sons of the pharaoh, performed by their fellow student, center, during a performance of the biblical story of Exodus at the Jewish Children's Museum in Brooklyn, New York. The three students were helping to tell the Passover story of how Moses led the Jewish people from slavery under the Egyptian pharaoh to freedom.

various afflictions would bring ruin on the Egyptians. At first the court magicians tried matching Moses and Aaron's power, but by the third plague they saw they were no match. Still, the pharaoh had not changed his mind about letting the Hebrews go. On being reminded by Moses after each plague about the imminent devastation of the Egyptians, Pharaoh would agree to let them go but would again take back his word. Finally God had told Moses that to punish the pharaoh for enslaving the Israelites, he would send a plague to Egypt to take the firstborn son and the firstborn animal from every household. God had instructed Moses that each Israelite family should sacrifice a lamb to be eaten during a special meal. The Israelites should then mark their doors with the blood of the lamb as a signal to the angel of death to pass over their homes during the plague. From this event comes the word *Passover*, or *Pesach* in Hebrew. It was only after this 10th plague (and losing his own son) that Pharaoh finally agreed to let the Hebrews go.

Since the Hebrews left in haste, they had no time to bake their daily bread in the usual way for their trip to Canaan; therefore they baked unleavened bread called matzo. Today Jews eat matzo during Passover in memory of the Exodus.

Celebrating Passover

The Jewish calendar, which has been used since 3761 B.C.E., is a lunar calendar with 12 months. Each month has 29 or 30 days, making a year 354 days long. To keep the fall and spring holidays in the correct seasons, an extra month is added every 19 years. For the Jews each day begins at sundown, or dusk, and lasts until the following sundown. Holidays on the Jewish calendar drift in a range on the Gregorian calendar.

Cleaning and Crumbs

Bread, cake, cereals, cookies, pizza, pasta, and beer are all considered *chametz*. Any food that has even touched these *chametz* is also *chametz*, even if it is by accident. Additionally, all dishware that is normally used throughout the year and that has come into contact with *chametz* must be thoroughly washed and put away during Passover. For this reason, many observant Jews keep a separate set of dishes and silverware that is used exclusively during Passover.

Passover begins on the night of the 15th day of the month of Nisan in the Jewish calendar (usually between the end of March and mid-April on the Gregorian calendar), and lasts for seven or eight days.

Passover is celebrated in Israel, home to almost half of the world's Jews, and in every country where Jews live, including the United States, Canada, Argentina, and parts of Europe. As Passover is celebrated in the home, Jews prepare for the holiday by purifying their houses.

Purifying the Home

Since the Hebrews were preparing to leave Egypt in a hurry, they made special bread of flour and water that would not need time to rise. Jews remember the Exodus by eating unleavened bread, or matzo, every year during Passover. Some Jewish families remove all *chametz* from their homes. *Chametz* includes any bread that rises in the oven, as well other foods made of grains, like wheat, barley, oats, and rye.

The removal of the *chametz* is also symbolic of the removal of self-centeredness and pride—or things that puff one up—from a person's soul. After the *chametz* has been removed, the house is often thoroughly cleaned as well. Jewish families may sort through their old or unused toys and clothes and decide which to donate to charity or to throw out as part of this thorough cleaning.

A Seder Dinner, Both Sacred and Scrumptious

After all *chametz* has been removed and the home has been thoroughly cleaned, Jewish families observe the first night (and sometimes the second night) of Passover with a special service and meal, the seder, during which the story of the Exodus is told. Usually the seder is led by one person, often the head of a family, such as the father or grandfather, or a special guest. Sometimes the story and the many rituals that accompany the seder are told by those at the Passover table.

Certain steps must be followed in order during the seder (in fact, the word *seder* means "order"). The steps that celebrants must follow are detailed in the Haggadah, a book filled with sacred passages, blessings, stories, songs, and psalms centering on the Exodus story. A Passover seder might last an hour or several hours, depending on how precise and thorough the leader is about following the rituals. Because Orthodox Jews strictly follow Jewish laws, they may hold a long seder, recited in

A traditional Passover seder plate is seen here at a Texas synagogue. The foods on the plate are symbols that help tell the biblical story of the Jews' escape from slavery in Egypt. Shown here, clockwise from top are horseradish root, symbolizing the bitterness of bondage; lamb shank, symbolizing the blood of the lamb painted on the doors of Jewish households; salt water, symbolizing the tears of the enslaved Jews; *charoset*, a fruit, nut, and wine mixture that represents the cement between the bricks that the Jews were forced to build with; matzo, which remembers the hurried flight of the Jews that gave them no time to allow the bread to rise; and the bitter herbs, symbolizing the bitterness of slavery.

The Passover seder is a Jewish ritual feast celebrating the biblical story of the Jews' escape from Egypt. Seder customs include drinking four glasses of wine, eating matzo, and partaking of symbolic foods placed on the Passover seder plate. The family here is dipping greens in salt water, which they then eat to symbolize the Jews' suffering in slavery.

Hebrew and Aramaic and include all the rituals. A seder for a secular (non-religious) Jewish family with young children might touch on the most important historical traditions, such as the Israelites' breaking free from slavery and leaving Egypt, but leave out numerous prayers and religious texts.

The Four Questions

A central part of the observance during the seder meal is the questions that are asked by the youngest child of a family (often the youngest son) and answered by the leader of the seder meal (or sometimes by all the other people present):

Why does this night differ from all other nights?
For on all other nights we eat either leavened or unleavened bread.

Bitter for Remembrance

The bitter vegetable (often horseradish) is known as *maror* and when it is eaten, Jews recite a blessing. The *maror* is usually eaten together with a relish of apples, nuts, wine, and cinnamon called *charoset*. This combination symbolizes the mortar that the enslaved Jews used to construct buildings for the Egyptians.

Why on this night only unleavened bread?
The unleavened bread is eaten because the Israelites had to flee Egypt quickly.

On all other nights we eat all kinds of herbs; why on this night only bitter herbs?
Jewish ancestors had been enslaved, which made their lives bitter.

On all other nights we need not dip our herbs even once; why on this night must we dip them twice?
The herb parsley is first dipped in salt or vinegar as a reminder of the greening that comes in the spring, and bitter herbs are then dipped in sweet sauce as a sign of hope—there was hope of freedom after the bitter years of slavery.

On all other nights we eat either sitting up or reclining; why on this night do we all recline?
Because on this night in olden times, reclining meant that you were a free man, not a slave.

These answers teach the youngest family members important historic and religious lessons.

Ashkenazi and Sephardic Jewish Traditions during Passover

By geographic origins, there are two major groups of Jews: the Ashkenazi Jews and the Sephardic Jews. *Ashkenazi* is an old Hebrew word for "Germany" and originally indicated Jews who spoke Yiddish, a German dialect. Today the Ashkenazi include Jews from Germany, France, and Eastern Europe and their descendants in the Americas. *Sephardic* is derived from the old Hebrew world for "Spain." The Sephardic

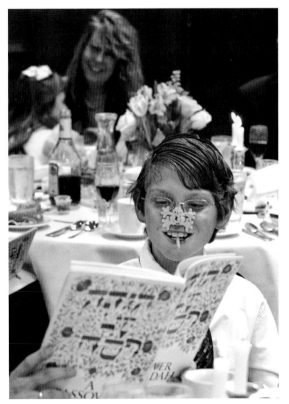

With a symbolic, nontraditional plastic frog on his nose, a boy sings from the Passover Haggadah during a seder meal in Richmond, Virginia. The frog symbolizes one of the 10 plagues unleashed on Pharaoh and the Egyptians, as described in the book of Exodus.

Jews are those who descended from Jews living in Spain and Portugal as well as northern Africa and the Middle East. Today, France is majority Sephardic since Sephardic Jews emigrated from northern Africa after the decline of the French empire in the 1950s and 1960s. Because Jews from these areas had been in countries controlled by the French, it was often relatively easy for them to adapt to French culture.

The differences between Passover celebrations among Ashkenazi and Sephardic Jews are most evident in the seder foods and traditions. For Ashkenazi Jews, in addition to *chametz,* foods classified as *kitniyot* by Ashkenazi rabbis centuries ago are also off limits on Passover. *Kitniyot* includes peanuts, beans, rice, dried fruits, and corn. For Sephardic Jews, dishes with these foods are not prohibited. Therefore, when Ashkenazi Jews make *charoset*, a fruit, nut, and wine mixture eaten during seder to represent the mortar (material that holds construction blocks together) used by the Jewish slaves in Egypt, it is almost always made with apples, walnuts, and red grape wine. On the other hand, Sephardic Jews use a wide variety of dried fruits, nuts, and often other liquids besides kosher grape wine.

During Passover, Ashkenazi Jews recite the 10 plagues that befell Egypt after the pharaoh refused to let the Israelites go. While the plagues are being described, the participants around the seder table dip their pinky finger into their wine glasses and let the drops fall on their plates. This ritual symbolizes the Jewish belief that everyone is a child of God, even the Egyptians.

Navruz

Navruz is the spring festival celebrated by people of the Zoroastrian faith, people originally from Persia (today's Iran), where Zoroastrianism was born, and in most countries located along the legendary Silk Road, an ancient trade route thousands of miles long that connects China with Asia Minor and the Mediterranean. The festival has been celebrated for nearly 3,000 years. The word *Navruz* means "new day" in Farsi, the language of the Persians. Zoroastrians consider Navruz the last of the seven stages of Creation. For the people in this region, Navruz is a celebration of nature's joyful awakening after the cold winter months. It is the start of planting, cultivating, and harvesting of crops, and a time of thanks, a day when conflicts and hostilities are forgiven and forgotten.

Origins of Navruz

Zoroastrianism

Zoroastrianism is based on the life of Zoroaster (believed to have lived around 1000 B.C.E.) who preached monotheism (belief in one God) in a land with a history of polytheism (the worship of many gods). Initially ridiculed for his teachings, Zoroaster eventually won over the king of

Zoroastrian Seven Stages of Creation

Zoroastrians believe the world was created in the following order:

1. The sky was created first, a stone sky that curved like a dome
2. Water filled the bottom of the dome
3. The Earth emerged from the water
4. In the center of the Earth grew the first plant
5. Near the first plant appeared the first animal, a bull
6. After the bull came the first human
7. Sun and fire were the final creations

Persia, and Zoroastrianism was the state religion of many Persian empires until the seventh century C.E. (the Common Era, which begins with the birth of Jesus).

Zoroastrianism is believed to be the oldest religion in the world that worships one God. Zoroaster taught that while there were other divinities, Ahura Mazda was the one uncreated God, and he made all that was good, including the other divinities. Zoroastrians believe in the central concepts of heaven and hell, the eternal struggle between good and evil, and a messiah who will save humanity.

According to ancient texts, Zoroastrians believed the world was created in seven stages. Each of these stages was historically celebrated with a feast day to honor the creations and to bring the Zoroastrian community together. However, the last and seventh creation, fire, was the most important of the celebrations, and is central to the Navruz festivities. Fire is sacred to Zoroastrians because it represents the force of life, with the Sun at its center. According to Zoroastrianism, fire purifies everything it touches: The universe was created by fire, is preserved by fire, and will be destroyed by fire. Ahura Mazda is venerated through sacred fire, which

Joining hands, Iranian men and women celebrate around a bonfire during Navruz, the Iranian spring festival and new year, in Tehran, Iran.

is believed to contain the prophet's presence. Because fire represents life, death, and rebirth, it is no coincidence that Navruz is celebrated during the spring equinox, the time of an ancient spring festival in pre-Zoroastrian times. Zoroastrianism is still practiced by close to 200,000 people today. Even in Iran, where it was once persecuted, it is now a protected minority.

Other Peoples Arrive and Celebrate

In ancient times during the Navruz festival, kings would wear crowns with images of the annual solar cycle on their heads and take part in the divine ceremony that was held in the Temple of Fire. There, they would celebrate and give their subjects gifts. As Turks and other wandering peoples ventured into Central Asia and areas around old Persia, they also began to observe Navruz. Navruz traditions became deeply rooted in the lives of European and Asian farmers, and it survived the arrival of Islam in the area some 1,400 years ago.

Navruz continues to be widely celebrated in Central Asian countries, where Muslims are a majority such as Azerbaijan, Afghanistan, Iran, Uzbekistan, Tajikistan, Kazakhstan, Turkmenistan, and Kyrgyzstan. It is also celebrated among the Kurds in Syria, Turkey, and Iraq. Those who follow the Baha'i Faith, a religion that took root in the 19th century and originated in Iran, also celebrate Navruz (though they call it Naw Rúz). During the late 20th century, many Central Asian republics made Navruz an official holiday.

A Turkish Kurdish woman with her daughter during a gathering to mark the spring festival of Navruz in Istanbul, Turkey.

Celebrating Navruz

When Navruz Is Celebrated

Navruz is celebrated each year on March 21 in the Northern Hemisphere, when the Sun enters the astrological sign of Aries. This date regularly corresponds with the spring equinox. In the Gregorian calendar, the spring equinox fluctuates between March 19 and 21. In some countries, the Navruz date has been changed to conform with the seasons and harvest cycles of that country. Whenever its precise start, Navruz marks the beginning of 13 days of observance of the Persian new year.

Spring Cleaning before the Morning "Star"

Navruz is traditionally a time to clean up. People clean their homes, wash draperies and rugs, adorn the house with flowers, and purchase new clothes. On Navruz, all housekeeping duties, including meal preparation and the cleaning of the house, should be complete before the morning "star" Venus appears in the sky (Venus is visible early in the morning during certain periods of the year).

Children eagerly await the arrival of Navruz because they receive gifts, money, and blessings from their elders on this day. When the day dawns, people greet one another with hugs, handshakes, and the words *Nowruz-e-tan Mubara* (Happy Navruz).

Prayer, Sacred Fire, and Offerings

For religious families, Navruz begins with a morning prayer offering thanks to God. They may then light a sacred fire and burn sandalwood and incense. In some countries, a family member or religious leader reads from the Avesta (the sacred book of the Parsee, a Zoroastrian group living in western India and descended from Persian refugees) while making symbolic offerings of fruit, water, and flowers.

Thirteen Days of Observance

During the 13 days of Navruz, families pay respect to relatives who have died. In some places, they also go to shrines of saints and holy men and light candles in their honor.

The Celebratory Table: Haft Seen

Zoroastrian customs require that the celebratory table, also known as Haft Seen, be displayed during Navruz. The Haft Seen table is central, as it is spread with symbolic elements, including several foods. On the Haft Seen table seven essential items are arranged. Their names begin with the letter *s* (*sin* in Persian) and commonly include:

> ## Visiting and Planting
>
> **People often visit relatives and friends in the days following Navruz; another custom is to plant seedlings of fruit trees.**

Seeb (apples), for beauty
Seer (garlic), to ward off ill-health and evil
Sabzeh (wheat sprouts), for the rebirth of nature
Sekkeh (coins), for prosperity
Serkeh (vinegar), for old age, maturity, and patience
Senjed (fruit of the lotus plant), for love
Sonbol (hyacinth), for happiness

A mirror, which reflects the past and reveals the future, and painted eggs, symbols of fertility and the sprouting of life, are also often placed on the table. These colorful spreads are tangible as well as palatable reminders of the deeper meaning of these spring traditions.

To celebrate Navruz, Iranians set the table of Haft Seen, denoting items beginning with the letter *sin* (S). In the center of this Haft Seen is a Quran surrounded by, clockwise from top, an apple, symbolizing beauty and health; sumac berries, symbolizing the color of the sunrise; coins, representing wealth; wheat sprouts, symbolizing rebirth; a bowl with goldfish, symbolizing life; decorated eggs, symbolizing fertility; fruit of the oleaster tree, symbolizing love; and garlic, symbolizing medicine.

The Mixed Traditions of Navruz

The sacred book on the Haft Seen table might be the Avesta, Bible, the Quran, or another holy book, as Navruz is not just a Zoroastrian holiday. Also, a portrait or image of Zoroaster, the founder of Zoroastrianism, might be displayed over the Haft Seen table. Some items on the table might vary for different celebrants based on different religious or cultural beliefs. Also, this tradition has evolved over time, depending on what materials were available in different regions of the world.

On the Haft Seen table, there are often lighted candles, since fire is sacred to Zoroastrians. Incense is burned to ward off evil spirits. Also commonly on the table are a bowl of rosewater, known for its magical cleansing powers, and a sacred book of scripture beside a water-filled vessel in which a live goldfish swims. The water and the fish represent a contented life that is active and productive.

The Last Day of Navruz

On the 13th day, ancient Persians believed they must be outdoors in order to avoid bad luck. In some areas, official outdoor picnics and celebrations take place in public parks and other open spaces. The 13th day is also sometimes a day to play pranks or tricks, not unlike April Fools' Day in the United States and Europe.

Holi

Among the many festivals celebrated in India, Holi is easily the most colorful and exciting, and children enthusiastically wait for its arrival. Also called the Festival of Colors, Holi is a Hindu spring festival that is celebrated for a two-day period starting on the full Moon day in the month of Phalguna, which is February or March in the Gregorian calendar. Holi marks the end of winter and the beginning of spring, as well as the flaming end of the Hindu demoness Holika. The holiday is observed with great joy throughout India and wherever Hindus live, such as Mauritius, off the coast of Africa; Nepal, Bangladesh, and Sri Lanka in South Asia; Guyana in South America; Great Britain in Europe; and the United States and Canada. Holi even offers a brief break from the strict caste system in Hindu society. Most of the year people are divided according to their ancestry and social class. But on Holi, everyone is equal.

Origins of Holi

The Legend of Hiranyakashipu

The festival of Holi originated in the ancient Hindu legend of Hiranyakashipu. It celebrates the triumph of good over evil. According to Hindu mythology there was a demon king in India named Hiranyakashipu, who wanted to avenge the death of his younger brother, also a demon, who had been slain by Vishnu (one of the trinity gods in Hinduism). In order to fight Vishnu, Hiranyakashipu sought to become the ruler of Earth, heaven, and the underworld, performing harsh penance and prayers for numerous years to please Brahma (the all-powerful creator) in order to obtain this power from him.

Students smeared with colored powder laugh during celebrations of Holi in Allahabad, India.

Finally Brahma gave the king his wish, but the demon king abused his new power, ordering everyone in his kingdom to worship him instead of Vishnu. The king's young son, Prahlada, was a devotee of Vishnu. Going against his father's wishes, Prahlada constantly prayed to Vishnu. Unable to make Prahlada change his ways, the demon king decided to kill him. The demon king asked his sister Holika (from whom the name of the festival is derived) to help him because she was sup-posedly impervious to fire. They planned to burn Prahlada to death and believed that she would survive while the little boy burned. So Holika sat on a burning pyre with her nephew Prahlada on her lap. Miraculously, Prahlada emerged unharmed by the flames and Holika, the demoness, was burned to death.

Holi Becomes Popular

According to Hindu belief, Krishna, a reincar-nation of Vishnu, is believed to have popular-ized the colorful tradition of Holi. The origin lies in Krishna's boyhood. Krishna used to indulge in pranks—his mischievous nature is legendary—by dousing the village girls with colors and water. Initially the girls were upset, but they were so fond of the boy that his popu-larity overcame their anger. Other boys joined in and made it a popular sport in that village. With time the tradition stretched to all regions of India, and, having survived through the ages, it has become a community festival for everyone.

Piles of colored powder for sale in a market in Mysore, India, during Holi.

A Pakistani Hindu celebrates Holi, the spring festival of colors, in Karachi, Pakistan. The bonfire in the background and colored powder smeared on her face are typical of the holiday's festivities.

Celebrating Holi

When Holi Is Celebrated

Like other Hindu festivals, Holi customs and traditions can differ significantly depending on the region. The length of the festival can also vary. In some places in northern India, Holi can last up to a week. In the state of Manipur in northeast India, it is a six-day festival. But in most places it is a two-day festival, starting on the eve of the bonfires and continuing the next day with the Festival of Colors. It always begins some time between the end of the February and the end of March.

On the Eve of Holi a Fire Is Lit

On the eve of Holi, also called Choti Holi ("Small Holi"), celebrants light bonfires on street corners to send away the cold dark winter nights and usher in spring. Hindus perform music, dances, and tell traditional sto-

Fortune-telling with Roasted Seeds

In some Hindu Holi celebrations, barley seeds are roasted in the fire and then "read" in order to see whether the coming harvest will be a good one. In other locations, it is the directions taken by the Holi bonfire flames that help predict the future. The fire cinders are also said to have healing powers, and Hindus sometimes take them from the dying fire at the end of the night to rekindle their own house fires.

Boys pour colored water on their friend during Holi celebrations in India. Holi, the Hindu festival of color, heralds the arrival of spring.

ries around the fires to celebrate Prahlada's miraculous survival and the death of Holika, his wicked aunt. People take cinders from this bonfire to rekindle their own house fires. The bonfires are generally made from cowdung cakes, logs of wood, honey, ghee (semifluid clarified butter), and harvest offerings.

Festival of Colors

In a tradition especially loved by children, Hindus gather during Holi to cover one another with colored powder, battle with squirt guns, and toss water balloons. On the streets of India during Holi, it is impossible to avoid a multicolored downpour.

Hindu lore offers at least three stories about the origins of the colored powder. According to one story, Krishna (a reincarnation of Vishnu) is believed to have popularized the colorful tradition of Holi when he would douse the village girls with colors and water. Another story holds that when Krishna was young, he often complained to his mother, Yashoda, about his companion Radha's light complexion and his own dark skin. Yashoda told him to put color on Radha's face and watch how the color of her skin changed.

Perhaps the most dramatic story associated with the origin of the powder on Holi involves the popular monkey god, Hanuman. One day, it is said, Hanuman swallowed the Sun, leaving the people in utter darkness.

The other gods, pitying the dejected people, suggested they rub color on each other to cheer themselves up. This they did, mixing the color with water and squirting each other gleefully. When Hanuman saw what they were doing, he could not help himself and let out a huge laugh, accidentally spitting out the Sun again and returning light and color to the world. All over India and the diaspora, these are a few of many stories told on this day to explain the remarkable and joyous Holi powders.

Conclusion

Whether inspired by nature, history, or religious feeling, spring festivals celebrate renewal. Symbols of purity or vitality—such as eggs, bright colors, and fire—are common elements of expression in the observance of spring holidays. Food, both its preparation and consumption, also plays a central role in the traditions and stories of spring holidays.

The ancient spring observances of Navruz and Passover share a few additional customs. Believers prepare for both holidays by thoroughly cleaning their homes. In both traditions, the ritual cleaning is both practical and spiritual. For Persians starting the new year clean means cleaning up relationships as well—paying off debts or apologizing to a friend or relative for a misdeed. For Jews, the ritual means removing all *chametz* from the home, as well as sorting out possessions that can be given to someone in need. Removing these things signifies the removal of pride so that Jews can go into Passover without selfishness and with a pure heart.

The festivals provide communities and families an opportunity to pass down traditions and stories from one generation to the next. Many of the stories retold during spring festivals contain an element of the triumph of good over evil, exemplified in the Resurrection of Christ, the Jewish liberation from slavery, the purifying element of fire in Zoroastrianism, and the triumph of Prahlada over his evil aunt Holika in Hindu mythology.

Girls throw flower petals during a Holi function in Calcutta, India.

Regional Traditions and Customs

◎ ◎ ◎

Africa

Various Christian European customs and religious beliefs found their way to the vast continent of Africa during the colonial era, especially sub-Saharan Africa. Likewise, much of northern Africa is Muslim due to its long-term trade arrangement with Middle Eastern neighbors to the north. Brought by Muslim traders and Christian colonizers and missionaries, Christianity and Islam retain a strong foothold in Africa. But long before these two monotheistic faiths were introduced, Africans believed in a supreme power that created the world. This supreme power has several different names and forms as varied as the thousands of cultures of Africa. In most African faiths, God is said to have created the Earth and then left the day-to-day workings to lesser gods, ancestral spirits, elders, rainmakers, and other mediators. Important tribal members who have recently died may also serve as spirits to whom the community gives offerings and prays—for a good harvest, more rain, or crop returns. The dead are also considered better able to speak to the spirits, helping to keep them pleased. Many Africans, even those who are Muslim and Christian, believe the dead must be taken care of by the living and that there is a connection between

An Apostolic minister splashes a man with water as he baptizes him during an Easter Sunday ceremony in Johannesburg, South Africa.

Africa's Many Drums

There are so many kinds of drums in Africa that to study them all would take decades. While some are used as musical instruments, others, called Talking Drums, are used to send messages up to 20 miles away. Certain African drums are only used for religious ceremonies. Others are used exclusively by the royalty of an African community. In Ethiopa, drumming is part of church ceremonies, but in much of western Africa ritual drums can only be used by selected people of a cultural or religious group.

the dead and the fertility of the land. To honor this connection, festivals are celebrated throughout Africa during planting and harvest seasons.

Spring celebrations in Africa are festive and sometimes intense, often with a mix of drumming, dancing, athletic contests, and ancient rites. Easter is celebrated in many parts of Africa. Like Christians in the rest of the world, African families go to church on Easter morning, decked out in new clothes and hats, ready to celebrate the renewal and rebirth of their faith, their God, and the land. In some countries of Africa, Easter festivities are blended with local rites and customs, such as traditional drumming and dancing. Also, in some villages, non-Christians are invited to Easter feasts in the homes of their Christian friends and relatives. While the Christian Easter is widely celebrated, parts of Africa also celebrate Navruz, and other spring rites. Other blended or distinctive springtime celebrations include those for Hili, Tafsit, and Sham El Nessim.

Camel Races during Tafsit in Algeria

During the colonial era, from 1830 to 1954, traders from Algeria, Libya, Niger, and northern Mali would meet in the Algerian town of Tamanrasset for a great festival. The main attraction was the camel race, with each tribe putting forth its best camel rider. The festival continues, though it has been modernized and renamed Tafsit, or the Festival of Spring. It takes place in April and its slogan is "friendship discovered" because it traditionally brought together traders from many places to celebrate the spring. Algerians love this festival, which enables people to gather and share various musical and cultural traditions. The camel race is still the main attraction.

A man arranges figurines and Easter eggs made of chocolate inside a shop in Abidjan, Côte d'Ivoire.

Easter in Côte d'Ivoire

For Christians in the western country of Côte d'Ivoire (Ivory Coast), Easter is a rare joyful time in the midst of a devastating civil war that began in 2002. Christians make up 20 to 30 percent of the more than 18 million living in Côte d'Ivoire. These Christians follow many Holy Week traditions. On Maundy Thursday they hold services in which devout Christians wash the feet of new believers in imitation of Jesus and his disciples. On Good Friday, some evangelical Christians go door to door in non-Christian communities to evangelize, or try to convert people to Christianity. Holy Saturday is a happy and spiritual time for Christians of Côte d'Ivoire, who stay up all night, dancing, singing, and praying until the dawn of Easter morning.

On Easter Sunday churches are decorated with ribbons to celebrate Jesus' Resurrection. Devout Christians attend church with friends and family. Singing and dancing are part of the celebrations, as people swing joyfully to the rhythm of drumbeats. After church, Christians share a special Easter dinner that consists of roasted or boiled rice served with meat.

Coptic Easter and Sham El Nessim in Egypt

Copts, as Egyptian Christians are known, celebrate Easter with great fervor. Copts identify strongly with Jesus' Crucifixion and Resurrection, as they themselves have been persecuted over the centuries for their

The Trouble with Chocolate

Almost half of the world's chocolate is made from cocoa beans grown in Côte d'Ivoire and other areas in western Africa. Some of the beans used to make chocolate Easter eggs are harvested by children who were sold into virtual slavery to farm owners who victimize starving families that desperately need money. Recently there has been international pressure on large companies that buy the Côte d'Ivoire cocoa, such as Nestlé, to make sure that there are decent labor conditions on the farms they buy from. In England, children recently protested child trafficking during the Easter holiday by holding Easter eggs and signs outside the headquarters of an international chocolate company. The signs read: "Warning—this product may contain the blood, sweat and tears of African child slaves."

beliefs. Coptic Easter, which occurs in March or April according to the Coptic solar calendar, is the most important feast for Coptic Christians. They spend the day with family and friends, often picnicking at sites such as the Urman Gardens in Cairo, Egypt's capital. In the 55 fast days leading up to Easter, and more than 150 other fast days during the year, Coptic Christians follow a vegan diet, excluding all meat products or foods that come from animals, even milk and cheese. Copts believe that the Bible instructs them to eat

Families walk in a park on the spring festival of Sham El Nessim in Cairo, Egypt.

vegan food during many fast days because it was the food eaten when God first created the world, before humans and animals began to reproduce and to live sinful lives.

On the first Monday after Coptic Easter, Muslims and Christians throughout Egypt celebrate Sham El Nessim, which means "sniffing the breeze." For more than 4,500 years this holiday has commemorated the start of the harvest season. In ancient times, salted fish, lettuce, and green onions were offered to the gods to ensure a good harvest. In modern-day Egypt, people enjoy picnics featuring traditional foods, including a variety of salted fish known as *fiseekh*. Just as in other spring celebrations, eggs are dyed in bright colors and symbolize the renewal of life.

Celebrate with Flames and Food in Ethiopia

Christianity spread throughout the eastern African country of Ethiopia in the fourth century, when two Christian brothers became stranded there and eventually converted the Ethiopian royalty. The Ethiopian Orthodox Church, associated with the Coptic Church of Egypt, is among the oldest Christian denominations in the world. Until 1975 the Ethiopian Orthodox Church was the state Church of Ethiopia. Though the Church's influence has declined in recent years, facing competition from Islam and Protestantism, 35 to 40 percent of Ethiopia's people still identify themselves as Orthodox Christian.

On the eve of Ethiopian Easter, called Fasika, Orthodox Christians attend midnight Easter services at which candles are lit. Easter concludes a 55-day fast during which Christians have eaten only one vegetarian meal a day.

After church on Easter, Christians break the fast by eating meat with pancakes made of *teff*, a grass flour, and by drinking honey wine or beer. Easter, like Christmas, is a time to gather with family and exchange gifts.

Bwiti's Blended Easter Customs in Gabon

While the western African country of Gabon is more than 55 percent Christian, many Christians there also practice the Bwiti religion, which blends Christian practices with an indigenous animist faith. Animism is the belief that plants, trees, and other things in nature, such as the sky, mountains, and rocks, have spirits or souls.

One Person, Many Faiths

Bwiti is a religion that blends animist beliefs with Christian ones. Bwiti is an open religion, and new converts can join more than one sect of the religion without conflict. There is no rivalry among the different sects, making it a uniquely tolerant religion.

The Bwiti Easter lasts for four days, beginning on Maundy Thursday and continuing until Easter Sunday. Devotees of the Bwiti religion eat *iboga*, a sacred hallucinogenic plant (or a plant that causes people to see things that are not actually there), during the evening rituals that are a part of the Easter celebration. Singing and dancing are central to the Bwiti Easter. The following day, Easter Monday, is widely celebrated among the Bwiti. As in many parts of the Christian world, egg-rolling competitions are a highlight.

Holi Celebrations in Mauritius

In Mauritius, a small island in the Indian Ocean off of South Africa, Holi is a major spring holiday. This is largely due to Mauritius's history. Mauritius was an uninhabited island before the arrival of the Europeans. The Dutch settled the island in 1598 and named it Mauritius after Prince Maurice of Nassau. France took possession of the island in 1715 and governed it until 1810, when British forces seized control. During British rule, in 1835, slavery was abolished and indentured laborers were brought from India. An entire society, from priests to business people to craftsmen and farmers, arrived at Mauritius from India. Over the next 200 years, these people practiced their Hindu faith on the isolated island, largely undisturbed by outside influence. Since 1948, when property qualifications were abolished and the franchise was made universal, the Indian community has dominated the legislature.

Today, Hindus, who now make up 48 percent of the population, celebrate Holi in Mauritius (now a republic in the British Commonwealth) as they would in India—with bonfires and colorful water fights. There is singing, dancing, and lots of music. It is a time for festive rejoicing. In the evenings, people visit each other's homes and exchange greetings.

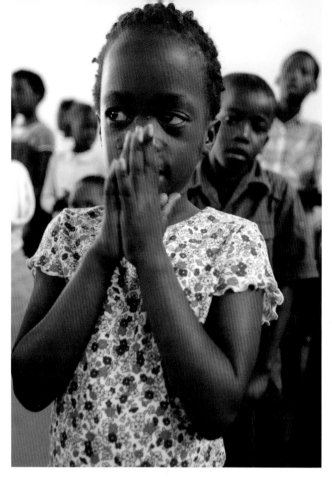

A child prays with others during an Easter ceremony at a church in South Africa.

Easter in South Africa

Christianity has a long history in South Africa. The country was colonized in the 17th century by the Dutch, who were seeking diamonds and gold and brought their Christian faith with them. Though Europeans no longer rule South Africa, Christianity has remained there. Denominations include the Zion Christian, which makes up 11 percent of the population, as well as Pentecostal, Catholic, Methodist, Dutch Reformed, and Anglican.

Together, Christian faiths make up close to 80 percent of the population. Of these faiths, the Zion Christian Church (known as the ZCC) has the most dramatic and elaborate Easter festivities. For several days, millions of church members travel to celebrate Easter in Zion City, home to the original founder of the Church, Engenas Lekganyane (ca. 1880–1948). Today the ZCC, founded and still led by black Africans, is one of the largest independent Christian Churches in the country.

The ZCC members believe in the power of their religion to heal. This can lead to troubles with traditional African healers, called *sangomas*. Yet despite occasional problems, the ZCC respects traditional African religious ways of life, especially the role of ancestor worship, the power of the ancestors to intervene on behalf of humans. South Africans can participate in ancestor worship and also be members of the ZCC. The members of the ZCC are proud that their religion was founded and is led by Africans and is an entirely black church that responds to black African needs. Unlike some Christian churches in African countries colonized by Europe, the ZCC's liturgy—or the form of worship that the Church allows—includes traditional South African singing and dancing.

Protestants and Catholics Come Together on Easter in Uganda

The eastern African country of Uganda is close to 33 percent Roman Catholic and 33 percent Protestant. In many parts of Uganda Protestants and Roman Catholics celebrate Easter together. Huge feasts are prepared and dishes made from goat meat are very popular. Many Ugandans visit their extended families in the countryside on this day. In church, prayers and the narration of Easter stories from the Bible are part of the Easter observance.

Mwaka Kogwa Means Navruz in Zanzibar

A unique Navruz celebration called Mwaka Kogwa takes place over a four-day period in Zanzibar, an island which is part of several islands off the east coast of Africa. Centuries ago Persians from southern Persia (now Iran) first arrived in Zanzibar and the other east African islands grouped with it. They came in order to escape hardship and famine and were the first group to settle Zanzibar in large numbers. Arabs in later years used the Zanzibar islands as a convenient trading base for their ivory and spices because the islands were small and easy to defend. Today, Zanzibar, part of the nation of Tanzania, is 99 percent Muslim and many old Persian traditions are still followed.

The Mwaka Kogwa festival is celebrated all over Zanzibar, including the larger islands of Unguja and Pemba, as well as smaller islands in the Zanzibar archipelago. The biggest and most famous celebration takes place in Makunduchi, in southeastern Unguja. Like Navruz celebrations elsewhere, during Mwaka Kogwa people believe that God and spirits help them purify the past year and welcome the new one. However, this New Year's celebration has taken on many traditions and customs of its own over the generations, including unique traditions that involve symbolic combat and a burning hut.

The highlight of Mwaka Kogwa is the ritual battle between two brothers chosen from northern Makunduchi and two brothers from southern Makunduchi who fight each other in the center of town on the first morning of the new year. Often former presidents or other dignitaries are guests of honor for this opening tradition.

During the mock combat, the brothers from the two parts of town hit each other with banana tree branches, because the branches split on contact. The combat follows rules passed down through the generations, until one side surrenders. Sometimes other townsmen enter the fight, and any boy who can keep up with the men, too, giving every male an opportunity to let out his grievances. The people of Zanzibar believe that this fight allows a fresh start in the new year and to let go of hard feelings. While the men fight, the women, dressed in their best attire, parade around the field and sing songs in Kikae, a local Swahili dialect. The songs which are about life and love, gently tease the men. Nowadays, the men tease back with songs of their own.

With the fight almost over, villagers build a pyramid-shaped hut out of coconut thatch and everyone's focus soon shifts to this hut. With the crowd gathered round, a local shaman (a spiritual guide and healer believed to be able to divine the future) enters the structure that is then set on fire by the crowd. With the hut fully ablaze, the shaman rushes out unharmed, and dives into a bush. The crowd then douses the hut's flames and everyone celebrates. It is believed that because the shaman is not hurt by the flames, no one will be hurt in the coming year if a house should catch fire.

When the mock fighting and hut burning is over, the celebrants go home and prepare for a huge feast. The cows, already butchered in preparation, will now be cooked. The villagers come back together for the feast, which is held outside. Everyone is welcome, family and strangers alike. In fact, people believe that a villager must share the meal with a guest in order to be happy on this day. Finally, people gather in their most colorful clothes to dance *ngomas*, the traditional dances accompanied by drums. The dancing often goes on all night.

Asia

Asia is the world's largest continent in size and holds almost three-fifths of the world's population. Many cultures and religions intermingle in this vast region. For instance, India, a country almost 81 percent Hindu, also has a significant Muslim population (about 14 percent), while Kazakhstan is more evenly divided between Muslims (47 percent) and Orthodox Christians (44 percent). Persian and Muslim influences are strong throughout Central Asia. In some areas, such as Turkmenistan and Azerbaijan, Muslims today make up more than 90 percent of the population, many of Persian ancestry.

From Easter in Macau, to Navruz in Kazakhstan, and Holi in Nepal, Asian spring festivals are a whirlwind of color, cuisine, and culture. In Hong Kong, Japan, Nepal, or Kyrgyzstan in the spring, the sweet and mellow aroma of incense hangs in the air, having been lit by families

People celebrate Holi in Madras, India, dousing each other with colored powder and water.

Artists march in a costumed procession during Navruz celebrations in Kazakhstan.

to purify their surroundings and send away evil spirits from the home or from beloved ancestors' graves. Dust fills the air too, from intense spring cleaning rituals before Navruz festivities in Central Asia.

The flames burn brightly around the spring equinox in India and Nepal, as Hindus joyously cast old objects into the Holika flames on the eve of Holi. Flames purify the Earth to ward off evil during a multitude of spring celebrations around Asia. And while eggs are often closely associated with Christian Easter and the Navruz Haft Seen table as symbols of rebirth and fertility, they are also tied to biblical stories involving Jesus' mother, Mary, in the Orthodox Armenian Easter.

Throughout Asia, spring is a time for friendship and the possibility of new love, as well as for a bit of healthy flirting among young adults. Food and gifts—either toys or treats to eat—play an important role in many Asian spring festivals.

Exciting Navruz Traditions

During ancient times in Central Asia, Navruz was observed in agricultural areas with bazaars, horse racing, festivals, and cockfights. The Uzbeks (people from Uzbekistan and neighboring areas) passionately adhere to their traditional dish *sumalyak*, a molasses-flavored cream of wheat prepared with flour and sprouted wheat grains. Sprouted grain is the symbol of life, abundance, and health.

The Face of Navruz

On Navruz in Afghanistan and other Persian-influenced regions, a folk character with a blackened face known as Haji Firuz serves as the official heralder of the new year. This comical character dressed in colorful clothes plays the tambourine and sings *"Haji firuze, sali ye ruze"* ("It is *haji firuz* time. It happens one day a year.") and other short tunes associated with Navruz. People gather around Haji Firuz to hear him sing. If they like his song and dance, the crowd throws coins and paper money.

In March, all over Central Asia houses and barns are cleaned to prepare for the Persian New Year and spring celebration of Navruz. When Islam first spread across Central Asia, Navruz was banned by some Muslim rulers because it was not originally a part of Islam. But people continued to celebrate, and eventually the ban was lifted. Navruz is widely celebrated in Iran (formerly Persia) and other countries with centuries-old Persian influence, such as Afghanistan, Azerbaijan, Kazakhstan, Kyrgystan, Tajikistan, Turkmenistan, and Uzbekistan.

As in other parts of the world where people of Persian descent have settled, Navruz in Asia begins with a thorough cleaning of homes and washing of draperies, tablecloths, and other household items. People also prepare by setting the Haft Seen table, lighting incense and candles in their homes to ward off bad luck and spirits, visiting the graves of their loved ones, eating special foods, and exchanging small gifts.

Navruz, a Revered Imam, and Red Flowers in Afghanistan

In Afghanistan, Navruz symbolizes happiness, peace, friendship, and reconciliation around the country. Afghans thoroughly clean their homes before Navruz to show their willingness to entertain the spirits of their ancestors. Some Afghans believe that Ajuzak, a threatening old woman, roams the countryside on Navruz. Rain on New Year's means that Ajuzak is washing her hair, a sign that the harvest of the coming year will be a rich one.

In the city of Muzar-e Sharif ("Tomb of the Saint") in northern Afghanistan during Navruz, a flag is raised at the shrine of Hazrat Ali. The city was founded in the 12th century after a local religious leader dreamed that Ali, son-in-law of the Prophet Muhammad, was buried there. Ali is known as Hazrat Ali in Afghanistan. Thousands of people visit the shrine hoping to touch the staff in order to be healed by its powers or to receive Ali's blessing.

During Navruz the Red Flower Festival is also held at Mazar-e-Sharif to welcome and celebrate the spring season. On the first day of spring, the meadows of Afghanistan are covered with wild red tulips (which give the festival its name), as well as poppies, daisies, and violets. Against the backdrop of the gorgeous mountains that divide the Kabul Valley, everyone gathers to enjoy picnics and kite-flying contests.

On the night of Navruz, Afghans often eat *sabzi chalau*, a spinach and rice dish that is sometimes served with lamb or chicken, and *samanak*, a sweet dish made especially for the new year that requires elaborate preparation. Two to three weeks before Navruz, wheat is planted in small pots. From this wheat young women make this sweet pudding that is meant to celebrate a good harvest and the beginning of the new year.

Easter in Macau, China

While Macau is 50 percent Buddhist, it is also 15 percent Roman Catholic, due to its colonization in the 16th century by the Portuguese. Today people in Macau attend church on Easter to celebrate the Resurrection. Children enjoy egg-rolling competitions on Easter Sunday and continue the festivities on Easter Monday by playing pranks and telling jokes.

The Special Status of Macau

As of 1999 Macau became what is known as a Special Administrative Region of China. China now has sovereignty over Macau, but for a period of 50 years Macau will keep a capitalist economy and some political independence, including the ability to elect local leaders and to travel freely. The government of China will control all foreign policy and decisions related to defense.

An Indian man shouts religious slogans during the Hindu festival of Holi, or festival of colors in northern India.

Holi Traditions in Hindu India

Depicting the rich variety of Holi celebrations in India is like trying to describe the view through a turning kaleidoscope—there are fascinating variations of scenes that all involve magnificent colors in endless entrancing patterns. In the northeastern region of Bengal Hindus place a statue of the deity Krishna, in his form as a child-god, in a cradle in front of the Holi bonfire. In Sri Dhama Mayapur, a town in West Bengal north of Calcutta, they also parade a statue of the saint of Bengal, known as Mahaprabhu Chaitanya, down the city's streets. In some parts of northern India, effigies (figures or carvings) of Holika are thrown into the bonfires. Newly harvested stalks are given as offerings to Agni, a fire God. In India Holi provides a great spring release as young men and women douse each other with color, or, in one tradition, engage in mock battles between the sexes.

In northern India, an exuberant tradition takes place every year in the small town of Barsana. Barsana is the home of Radha, the teenage love of Krishna. Not far away is the town of Nandgaon, Krishna's hometown. One week before Holi starts in the rest of India, the young men from Nandgaon converge on Barsana and try to raise a flag over the Hindu temple there. As the men run through town in large groups, the women of Barsana clobber them with sticks, trying to capture them and prevent them from reaching the temple. The men wear foam pads to protect their bodies, but they are not allowed to strike back. The women punish the men they capture by dressing them in saris, the traditional women's dress of India. The "prisoners" are also dolled up with women's makeup and commanded to dance.

The following day, Barsana's men take revenge by going en masse to Krishna's town of Nandagaon. Now the women of this town get to flog the Barsana men. It is all in good fun, as the tourists who attend can clearly see. The festival concludes on the third day in a special temple nearby where numerous celebrations take place, including playing Holi (the act of decorating oneself or others in color) with pink and white powder.

Celebrating Shunbun Hi in Japan

Near the time of the spring equinox falls the Japanese holiday of Shunbun Hi. This is a time taken for people to show affection toward other living beings and express their oneness with nature. Many people also visit the graves of their loved ones, clean them up, place flowers on them, light incense sticks, and pray for the deceased.

Easter Red Egg Greeting in Kazakhstan

In Kazakhstan, more than 40 percent of the population is Russian Orthodox. An Eastern Orthodox Church led by a Russian patriarch, the Russian Orthodox Church has roots in the Church of the Byzantine Empire (or the Eastern Roman Empire). Easter is called Holy Paschal and is observed on the second Sunday in April of the Julian calendar. In Kazakhstan on the eve of Easter, people cook special dishes, bake rich Easter cakes, such as *kulich* (a Russian Easter bread), and paint Easter eggs.

The egg is the main Paschal symbol of Resurrection. When people give each other the Paschal greeting, they also exchange eggs that are dyed red to symbolize the blood that Jesus shed to atone for the sins of the world. On Easter the eggs are brought to church to be blessed.

Easter Sets the Whole Calendar

The Russian Orthodox ecclesiastical calendar for each year is based on the date of Easter, which is arrived at using an algorithm, or step-by-step process for solving a math problem. Once the date for Easter has been set, most of the remaining religious observances can then be determined.

During Paschal Week people feast on meat, eggs, and other rich foods that were not allowed during the preceding 40-day Lenten fast. Their celebratory tables overflow with many delectable dishes.

Sugar and Spice for Navruz in Kazakhstan

In Kazakhstan, people welcome the spring by asking forgiveness for their sins, paying off old debts, and renewing friendships. Seven is a significant number during Navruz, and so everyone visits seven houses and invites seven guests to their homes. During this festival people play games and sports matches. The Kazakhs are known for their ability to ride horses. One sport, called *kazakhsha-kyres,* requires men to wrestle one another while each contestant is mounted on a horse. The first one to pull the other off his horse wins. In another sport, *kokpar,* teams of men on horseback compete to capture a slaughtered goat's body. Navruz is a joyous time in Kazakhstan, marked by parties, dance, drama, and music festivals. Festive Navruz dishes include sugared wheat porridge and cinnamon-spiced veal.

Called *kokpar* in Kazakhstan and *buzkashi* in Afghanistan, Afghans shown here in Kabul, Afghanistan, play the game of goat dragging with two teams of horsemen competing to throw a beheaded calf, goat, or sheep, as the ball, into a scoring circle. The sport is played throughout Central Asia, particularly during Navruz celebrations in spring.

Childhood on Horseback

In Kazakhstan, there is a saying that Kazakh children learn to ride horses before they learn to walk. Not only during Navruz but also in practically every Kazakh holiday, horses play a role. Indigenous Kazakhs were originally nomadic, traveling hundreds of miles with their flocks of sheep, camels, goats, and horses. Though the Kazakhs no longer roam the great distances they once did, the horseback-riding skills that they originally developed to survive are still central to their culture.

Mountain Juniper and Mutton for a Memorable New Year in Kyrgyzstan

When celebrating Navruz in Kyrgyzstan, people purify their homes by burning mountain juniper twigs to drive away evil spirits. They cook dishes

including pilaf, boiled mutton (sheep meat), and *kok-samsa,* which are pies filled with spring greens and the young sprouts of steppe (prairie land) grasses. Traditionally people attempt to fill up their tables with as many dishes as possible because they believe that doing so will bring them success and plenty during the coming year. Navruz is also marked by national singing and storytelling contests, horseback competitions, and outdoor celebrations.

Children perform during Navruz celebrations in Bishkek, Kyrgyztan.

The White Month Brings Spring in Mongolia

In Mongolia, the lunar New Year is called Tsagaan Tsar. Its exact date depends on the cycles of the Moon and can fall anytime between the end of January and early March. Tsagaan Tsar means "the white month," the color white standing for purity, happiness, wealth, and well-being. Tsagaan Tsar is the start of the milk-producing and breeding period of cattle, and people hope that spring will bring an abundance of dairy products. Families start planning for the holidays a month in advance by cooking lots of food, purchasing gifts, and cleaning out their homes and sheds. Women also make clothing for the family to wear on Tsagaan Tsar. During the Tsagaan Tsar festivities, celebrants throw red dough representing their enemies (or the enemies of Buddhism) into huge bonfires.

The New Year's Eve of Tsagaan Tsar is called Bituun and is the time when family and friends eat the last dinner of the old year. This meal often includes sheep's head or lamb's meat. Each family prepares the most lavish meal possible and friends and family exchange food dishes. On this night in some regions, it is common to visit the family of married daughters. The following morning, everyone wakes up early to greet the rising Sun, and then family members exchange greetings and gifts, usually something modest such as socks, or a drink. Mongolians then celebrate the New Year for three days or more, eating foods such as dumplings called *buuz* and sheep's back and tail. They drink fermented mare's milk, vodka, or *tsagaalga,* which is a milk drink with rice.

It is said that at Bituun a local goddess called Baldanlham is riding her horse during this period and that she will come by each house three times. Every family sets out three pieces of ice for her horse to drink. On Tsagaan Tsar, as on other Mongolian holidays, people sing songs and play games. In ancient times and still today, the men of the family take their children to an *ovoo*, an arrangement of stones on a hilltop, with trays of food and other offerings to show their gratitude to nature.

The Flour Forecast

Mongolians believe that if there is more meat in the *buuz* (dumplings) than flour, the family will have enough clothes in the coming year. If there is more flour, a family will have enough food. If there is the same amount of meat and flour, everything will be right for the year.

Holi Lasts a Whole Week in Nepal

Hindus make up more than 80 percent of Nepal's population. In Nepal the weeklong Holi celebration is called Rung Kelna, or "playing with color." The night before Holi begins festival-goers light huge bonfires and burn images of Holika to cleanse the area of evil spirits and to symbolize Holika's death.

The next day the *chir* (or *chit*) pole—a greased pole decorated with colorful flags—is set up at Durbar Square in Kathmandu to mark the beginning of the festival. People wear old clothes because old and young alike throw water balloons and colored powder at one another throughout the day. In other parts of Nepal the festivities revolve around a 25-foot-tall umbrella. At its base people light sticks of incense and leave flowers and red powder. Then they toss water-filled balloons out of upper windows, a clever way of drenching someone else without risking retaliation.

The last day of the festival is a wild one indeed. Young men cover themselves with red powder and arm themselves with water pistols, water balloons, and more colored powder as they wander the streets of the city, making themselves targets for the multitudes.

Easter in the Philippines

Due to the influence of Catholic Spain in colonial times, the Philippines is more than 80 percent Roman Catholic. In the Philippines people attend midnight prayer services for Easter and celebrate Jesus' Resurrection by lighting candles. Christians parade through

An image of the "Risen Christ" is paraded during Easter Sunday rites in Manila, Philippines.

the streets pulling *carrozas* (carts) carrying elaborate full-sized figures from the Easter story, including Mary, Jesus, Judas, and Pontius Pilate, among others. These processions are also popular in Spain and in Latin America, which was colonized by Spain even before the Philippines.

Navruz Marriage Traditions in Turkey

Turkey's Navruz customs are quite exceptional. In many parts of the country on the night of Navruz, young men who want to get married eat half a *tuzlu gyllyk*, a special pastry made from salted wheat dough. After eating, they do not drink water so that they go to bed thirsty, believing that they will marry the woman who offers them water in their dreams. On the following day they place the remaining half of the *tuzlu gyllyk* on the roof or chimney of their homes. If a crow takes the dough and flies away with it to another rooftop to eat it, then the man will marry the daughter who lives in that house. But if the crow grabs the pastry and flies away without stopping, the man will marry a woman from a faraway land.

In the Kars region of northeast Turkey on the evening of Navruz, young unmarried men and women gather at one house and send a child to fetch a bucket of water. After the child returns, the men toss colored threads into the bucket, and the women throw in pins. It is believed that those whose threads and pins become intertwined will marry each other.

Celebrating the Rainy Spring Season in Southeastern Turkmenistan

In some areas of Turkmenistan, Navruz celebrations are directly tied to the rebirth of the land and to farming. Turkmen, who make up 75 percent of the population, observe two distinct Navruz periods in the southeast of the country, one related to breeding cattle that takes place in February, and a longer one related to agriculture, Ypek Navruzi, in March.

The Persian-speaking population of southern Turkmenistan celebrates the new year's holiday as Navruzi Eid. During the holiday, people attend open-air fairs, where they build swings, cook various dishes, and paint eggs. On Navruz they boil a meat soup of wheat barley and dress it with yellow raisins and other dried fruits. During Navruz Eid, celebrants visit their friends and relatives, bringing food as a gift. Other Turkmen people celebrate with music, plays, traditional games, sports, beauty contests, poetry nights, and other activities.

Europe

Easter is the spring festival most widely celebrated throughout Europe, and here, perhaps more than anywhere else in the world, it is clear that Easter is both a holy day that celebrates Jesus' Resurrection and a spring celebration with ancient pagan roots.

All over Europe (especially in the north), as well as areas of European influence such as the Caribbean, people play egg-rolling and other egg-related games that take place on the day after Easter to commemorate the rolling away of the rock from the mouth of the cave where Jesus was buried. In England, Germany, and Ireland children roll colorfully died, hard-boiled Easter eggs down green, grassy slopes. The child whose unbroken egg reaches the end of the slope first is declared the winner. In another game, two opponents battle by knocking hard-boiled eggs against each other. The winner receives the loser's broken egg and sometimes another small gift from the host of the event. All across Europe people light candles as part of their Easter celebration.

As in many parts of the Christian world, the Easter hare brings European children baskets full of small toys and candy on Easter morning. The hare also takes charge of hiding the Easter eggs around the gardens, yards, and parks of Europe for children to find. Like the egg itself, hares and rabbits are ancient signs of fertility.

In some parts of eastern Europe people celebrate Easter Monday through a raucous tradition with ancient roots. It is in part a

A girl rolls a boiled egg during traditional Easter festivities in the old city of Riga, Latvia.

Religion and European Geography

People of many faiths live in Europe, with the largest groups being Orthodox Christians in Eastern Europe; Roman Catholics, largely in southern Europe and Ireland; and Protestants in northern Europe. On Easter morning, Christians all over Europe go to church and listen to their priests or pastors give sermons about the story of Jesus' Resurrection. In many countries, people decorate eggs, often red to symbolize the blood of Jesus, and give them as gifts to family and friends. The eggs symbolize the rebirth of Christ and the rebirth of the land in the spring. Churches are draped in spring flowers, and congregants dress up in their finest clothing. After church, families and friends gather to eat large Easter feasts, often with sweet bread and lamb, since Jesus is described as the Sacrificial Lamb or Lamb of God, who died for all of the world's sins.

flirting ritual (like some Holi traditions) where men gently whip women or pour water on them to ward off evil spirits.

While the majority of the European population is Christian and Easter is the spring festival most widely celebrated throughout Europe, Jewish people also live all over Europe and celebrate the spring observance of Passover. There are more than 1.5 million Jewish people living in Europe, with more than 1 million in the European Union countries. The largest Jewish populations live in France (more than 600,000) and the United Kingdom (275,000). Outside of the European Union, Russia has the largest Jewish population, at close to 265,000 people.

In addition to Easter and Passover, many European countries also celebrate Labor Day (or May Day), as a spring festival in early May. While Labor Day is a holiday to honor the rights of workers throughout the world, many parts of Europe combine this observance with ancient rites and customs to welcome the warm weather and celebrate the fertility of the Earth. Labor Day festivities that celebrate spring are especially common in northern Europe, where it is often just beginning to warm up in early May. Other festive aspects of spring observances include festivals such as Martenitsa, the Bulgarian holiday involving the wearing of little dolls for good fortune.

Lighting Candles in Andorra

In Andorra people light candles during a vigil and at midnight services the night before Easter. Then on Easter they light a special candle to signal Jesus' Resurrection. That candle is lit every day for the next 40 days until Ascension Day—the day that marks Jesus' Ascension to Heaven—when it is finally put out.

Martenitsi Dolls Help Usher in the Spring in Bulgaria

Bulgarians celebrate a unique spring festival called Martenitsa on the first day of March, which they consider the beginning of spring. On

this day, Bulgarians wear small, woven red-and-white woolen dolls, either on their wrists or fastened to their clothes. Called *martenitsi*, the dolls represent happiness and prosperity. The red and white colors on the dolls represent the purity of the white snow that will soon be gone and the onset of spring, with its sunny days. Bulgarians are supposed to wear these dolls until they see a stork, which is thought to be the sign of spring. In some areas, people tie the *martenitsi* on a fruit tree

Bulgarian *martenitsi*

to transfer their good luck and prosperity to the fruit-bearing tree. On Easter, like other Europeans who use candles in their Easter observance, Bulgarian Christians hurry into the streets after midnight mass with burning candles in their hands.

Gingerbread Lambs and Spirited Rituals in the Czech Republic

In the Czech Republic, families bake gingerbread in the shape of a lamb for Easter dinner. Young girls also decorate Easter eggs, which they give to boys on Easter Monday when the boys come to the girls' homes to sing hymns. A nationwide contest is held to select the most beautifully decorated Easter eggs. Family and friends exchange red eggs to wish one another happiness, good health, and prosperity.

In the Czech Republic Easter Monday is also known as the day of *pomlazka* (whip). Since pagan times men have used their *pomlazkas* to ward off evil spirits by whipping girls and livestock on the legs. Today young boys gently whip girls on their legs and douse them with water. While whipping them, the boys sing an Easter song asking the girls to give them Easter eggs. As a reward for protecting her against evil, a girl hands an Easter egg to a boy and ties a ribbon on his *pomlazka*. Today, girls also give ribbons, bread, and brandy as signs of gratitude.

Easter Poetry Riddles in Denmark

In Denmark children send *gækkebrev*—anonymous letters written in poetic form—to their family members on Easter. The letter is often a beautiful paper cutout with words written in the middle. Recipients have to guess the names of the *gækkebrevs'* writers. If the recipients do not guess correctly within a period of time, they have to give the senders decorated chocolate Easter eggs. The Easter celebrations continue through Easter Monday, a public holiday in Denmark.

Vappu in Finland

In Finland, Labor Day is celebrated with Vappu, an ancient spring festival. It is a time for workers to conduct parades and rallies and for Finns to herald the arrival of spring, though it may still be snowing. Street

Priests and devotees gather around a ceremonial fire during an Easter vigil ritual in front of the Notre Dame Cathedral in Paris. The ritual symbolizes the Resurrection of Jesus that is represented by light overcoming darkness.

carnivals, feasting, and drinking mead (liquor made with honey) are highlights of the day.

Easter in France

In France families dress in their best clothes to attend church on Easter. Afterward they share large meals and children receive specially decorated chocolate Easter eggs from their parents and grandparents. Feasting and exchanging greetings and Easter eggs continue through Easter Monday the next day.

Mary Celebrated in France

In France, Labor Day is also the Day of the Lily of the Valley, devoted to Jesus' mother, the Virgin Mary. French workers hold marches and rallies throughout the country on this day while also honoring Mary by exchanging gifts and lilies of the valley.

Fertility and Workers Honored in Greece

In Greece, May 1 honors workers and celebrates fertility and spring. With schools and workplaces closed, Greek families take time out for picnics, and children collect wildflowers to make wreaths. The wreaths adorn front doors until August 29, the Feast of St. John, when they are burned in bonfires.

Another Meaning for Eggs in Hungary

Early Sunday morning, children awake to find small gifts of candy and toys beside their beds. A traditional breakfast of Easter eggs, ham with horseradish, braided cake bread, and hot chocolate follows. Horseradish is eaten with the Easter breakfast ham because the overpowering odor of horseradish is traditionally thought to ward off evil. According to legend, babies who eat horseradish will not get colic, a stomach pain that leads to uncontrollable crying.

On Easter Monday, traditionally young men would pour buckets of water over young women's heads to ward off evil and protect them from harm. The women rewarded the men with kisses and eggs painted red, the color of passion. Today, instead of pouring water, they spray perfume and exchange painted and chocolate eggs.

The Earth Is Still Frozen on the Day of the Resurrection in Iceland

Easter egg hunts do not take place in Iceland because the land is generally covered with snow and the weather is extremely cold. Instead, children receive chocolate-filled eggs and fortune cookies on Easter. Easter dinner usually consists of pork, peas, carrots, jelly, and red wine. Feasting and the exchange of greetings continue on Easter Monday.

Spark Sunday in Liechtenstein

In Liechtenstein winter is chased away in a flaming ceremony known as Funkensonntag, or Spark Sunday. On this day, many residents observe a pre-Christian tradition of burning an effigy (a model or statue) of winter in the form of a witch, to banish the cold and welcome spring. People build bonfires by piling fir trees into a tower on which the winter witch is placed for Spark Sunday. When the tower is lit just after dark on this dramatic night, the fir wood creates magnificent sparks.

Easter Granny in Lithuania

Earlier on Sunday, after the Easter church service, the woman of the house shells a blessed Easter egg and, after breaking it carefully, hands a piece to each family member to ensure that there will always be love and peace in the family. Children hunt for colored eggs, which are not hidden by the Easter Bunny, but rather the Easter Granny, known as Velyku Senele. Children are told that Velyku Senele travels across Lithuania in a cart led by Easter bunnies and stops at homes to place decorated eggs and sweets either in the yard or in special Easter baskets. Only those children who have behaved well are rewarded with sweets and brightly colored eggs, while those who have been bad receive a single white egg.

Easter's Dark Beginnings in Malta

In Malta, Easter Eve celebrations begin in complete darkness. Then at a chosen hour, church bells break the silence of the night, and the churches are illuminated with chandeliers, candles, and floodlights announcing Jesus' Resurrection. Families exchange gifts, especially *figolli*, a special pastry shaped like a person, dove, fish, or basket. The pastry is filled with marzipan—a sweet concoction of ground almonds and sugar—and coated with icing or chocolate. Over the next few days a local priest visits the parishioners to bless the village homes and pass out olive leaves. This tradition began in ancient times, when people used to burn these olive leaves in order to ward off evil spirits.

From Darkness, Light in Moldova

On Easter Eve in Moldova, a midnight liturgy begins in solemn darkness. Then the priest lights the congregants' candles, as a symbol of their belief in Jesus'

A girl lights candles during Easter in a Serbian Orthodox Christian Church, in downtown Belgrade.

Resurrection. Easter Sunday afternoon the faithful gather again for prayer with lighted candles and greet one another joyously, saying: "Christ is Risen," the Easter salutation, which is answered, "Truly He is Risen."

An Easter Bonfire in the Netherlands

On Easter, devout Dutch Catholics attend Mass in their local churches. A beautiful Easter wreath hangs on every door, and homes are decorated with spring flowers. In the rural areas, almost every village celebrates Easter by lighting a bonfire on a hill or a high piece of land. Each village tries to outdo the others with the biggest bonfire, for which villagers collect wood long in advance.

The Emmaus Festival in Poland

On Holy Saturday Polish families take baskets of food to be blessed. These baskets contain *kielbasa* sausage, eggs, Polish bread called *babka*, salt, pepper, and often a little sculpture of a lamb (usually made out of sugar) with a flag showing the cross, symbolizing Jesus. These ingredients are used to prepare the Easter meal on Sunday. In addition, ham, white sausage, smoked bacon, cheesecake, and lamb-shaped cake, are very popular.

On Monday in Kraków, Catholics celebrate the ancient festival of Emmaus, commemorating the risen Christ's encounter with two of his disciples on the way to the town of Emmaus. On this day in ancient times young men fought each other with sticks, trying to show off their strength to young women. Many men also courted women by gently hitting them with willow twigs.

More commonly celebrated on Easter Monday is a Polish tradition called Smigus Dyngus, or "Wet Monday." On this day boys douse girls with water using squirt guns and buckets. The more a girl is drenched, the more likely it is that she will get married. Girls get their revenge the following day, when they can spray the boys as much as they would like.

A priest blesses samples of food brought in baskets by parishioners in a Warsaw church on Easter Saturday in Poland.

Easter Monday is a time for religious parades as well. During these parades celebrants carry holy pictures throughout the city, accompanied by bands and church choirs. Children are given sweets and toys on this day.

Candles in Romania

In Romania during the Easter Eve service, candles are lit for every person in the community and remain lit throughout the night. Romanians believe that the light of the candle protects people against being struck by lightning on their way home.

Jews Celebrate Passover Openly in Russia

When Russia was part of the Soviet Union, Russian Jews had to celebrate Passover in secret, for fear they would be punished or even jailed. Under Soviet rule, and especially between the end of World War II in 1945 and the end of the Soviet Union in 1992, all religion in Russia was suppressed. Until recently, some Russian Jews had never celebrated Passover and were unfamiliar with its rituals and traditions. Today, and since the fall of the Soviet Union, new synagogues are being constructed in Russia. In these synagogues and other community centers, Jewish leaders are helping elderly and middle-aged Russian Jews to better understand their history and traditions through lectures, movies, meetings, and plays. Local schools are also being brought into the fold and Jewish children are learning about the Passover traditions that have not been openly practiced since their great grandparents were alive. Many Russian Jewish synagogues and organizations are also holding community Passovers to bring Russian Jews together.

Sprinkling Day in Slovakia

In Slovakia the ancient tradition of symbolically pouring water on young women to ward off evil spirits is referred to as Sprinkling Day, and on Easter Monday young men and boys are free to pour water on single and married women alike. The girl or woman gives a colored egg to the boy or man to thank him for driving away the evil spirits.

Egg Superstitions in Slovenia

In many parts of Slovenia, hens are fed Easter eggs, which are believed to make them lay more eggs. Some Slovenians also stick eggshells on their ceilings to drive cockroaches away, while in other regions people scatter Easter eggshells around their homes to keep snakes away.

Effigies and Easter Parades in Spain

On Easter Sunday some of the faithful in Spain make an effigy, or rough model, of Judas (or some unpopular politician) out of straw and burn it. Judas is the disciple who betrayed Jesus to the Romans. Spanish Christians also perform dramatic reenactments of other important Easter stories. In one, a child dressed as an angel is lowered from the sky by a rope to remove the veil covering the Virgin Mary's face, reenacting the angel's appearance before Mary after her son's Resurrection. Spanish families then gather to celebrate Jesus' Resurrection and sing traditional Easter hymns. They also march in colorful parades (*cofradia*) with magnificent floats. Easter Monday is a day for egg-decorating contests, music, and feasting—especially on chocolate buns and cakes.

Easter in Sweden

On Easter Sunday in Sweden people give each other beautifully decorated Easter eggs. In a slight variation on the egg-rolling tradition, children roll hard-boiled eggs down a roofing tile, held slanted onto the floor. If the egg hits another egg, the child gets to keep

A set of effigy sculptures for the parade at the Fallas Festival in Valencia, Spain, to mark the beginning of spring. As the finale of the festival, sculptures and effigies made of wood and other flammable materials are burnt to welcome the coming of spring.

both eggs. While some egg-related games take place on Easter Sunday, most are played on the Monday after Easter, which is a national holiday throughout Europe.

Eiertütschen in Switzerland

On Easter in Switzerland entire families gather to celebrate the Resurrection of Jesus. Children receive specially decorated Easter eggs made of chocolate from their parents and grandparents. In the mountain valleys of Switzerland, where winter lasts for more than six months, Easter not only signifies the Resurrection but also the reawakening of nature. This rebirth of life is celebrated by sharing wine and blessed bread and donating gifts to the poor—a tradition, called Osterspende, that has been followed since the 16th century. In Switzerland dining and exchanging greetings and Easter eggs continue on the next day, Easter Monday. The custom of egg cracking, known as Eiertütschen locally, is extremely popular. In the towns of Frümsen, Oberriet, St. Gallen, and Effingen, in the canton of Aargau, the custom of egg throwing takes place every Easter Sunday or Monday. The participants in this game throw the brightly colored eggs at spectators, who retaliate by eating them right away. This festive day ends with music and dance.

Easter Egg Traditions in the Ukraine

Perhaps the most beautiful and carefully designed Easter eggs in the world can be found in the Ukraine. In a process called *pysanky*, which means to design or to write, Ukrainians use a stylus filled with melted wax to draw intricate pat-

Ukrainian Easter eggs decorated by *pysanky*, a traditional process that dates back more than 2,000 years.

terns on the eggs. Then when the egg is dipped into dye, the wax resists the dye. This process is repeated many times for each egg. By the end the egg is multicolored and beautiful.

In the past, all *pysanky* dyes came from natural materials such as boiled onion skins or buckwheat husks, black hollyhocks or birch leaves. Since these are natural dyes, the colors are muted and earthy, rather than bright or pastel like the colors often seen on North American Easter eggs. The colors and designs also have meanings associated with them. For example, a design of pine needles symbolizes health, endurance, and youth, while a ladder stands for prayer and prosperity. Green means spring, hope, and new growth. White represents purity, innocence, and birth. Today, *pysanky* artists have fun experimenting with new technology and new dyes. They can buy electric styluses that maintain the wax at the perfect temperature and use colors that were unavailable previously.

Originally, these dyed eggs were part of pagan rituals. The *pysanky* designs reflected nature: the Sun, plants, animals, and weather. After the introduction of Christianity, *pysanky* became associated with Christ's Resurrection in addition to the return of spring. Christian symbols were added to the repertoire, and new materials were introduced. For example, some artists dip the eggs in a light coating of wax and then press beads into the wax before it cools. Thus, each *pysanky* is individual, reflecting the artistic preferences of each artist, and the special meanings that he or she wishes to express.

Hot Cross Buns and Rolling Eggs in the United Kingdom

Hot cross buns!
Hot cross buns!

A baker arranges hot cross buns in London.

> One a penny, two a penny,
> Hot cross buns!
> If ye have no daughters,
> Give them to your sons.
> One a penny, two a penny,
> Hot cross buns!

England is home to many happy Easter traditions. On Easter Monday egg-rolling competitions are held in parks all over England often to the sound of live jazz music. After rolling decorated hard-boiled eggs down hills to see who wins, children can stroll through a fair featuring craft stalls and games.

Hot cross buns are characteristic of Easter in England. Consisting of sweet bread made with yeast and decorated with an icing cross, these buns are believed to have originated in pagan times. The buns became associated with the Roman Catholic Church in the 14th century when monks started giving them to the poor on Good Friday. When Henry VIII broke with the Roman Catholic Church, he wanted to ban the tasty buns too, but the English people would not give them up. In the 16th century, Queen Elizabeth I passed a law that allowed their sale, but only on Easter and Christmas. Hot cross buns are still traditionally eaten on Easter Eve wherever Britons live.

Latin America and the Caribbean

Because it is located in the Southern Hemisphere, September, October, and November are spring months in Latin America. Still the months of March and April bring celebrations of many faiths. Processions and passion plays proclaim the Christian Holy Week all over Central and South America, while English-influenced Easter celebrations take place alongside Hindu Holi festivities in parts of the Caribbean. In March or April every year in Argentina, a large and long-established Jewish community celebrates Passover in both the Buenos Aires capital, and on cattle ranches in the countryside. In addition, a modern version of an ancient celebration takes place during the spring equinox, which brings together local Mayans and tourists to remember and re-create the traditions of the ancient groups of Mesoamerica.

A huge majority of Latin America has practiced Roman Catholicism since Spain first conquered and colonized most of this diverse continent more than 500 years ago. But Spain was not the only European nation that sought Latin America's vast mineral, agricultural, and human resources so many years ago. The English also colonized parts of the Caribbean and South America, as did the Portuguese in Brazil. This influence can still be seen today. In the Bahamas, for example, hot cross buns and egg-rolling competitions are still popular.

Churchgoers carry a statue of Jesus resurrected during an early morning Easter procession in Paraty, Brazil.

The British also brought indentured servants from India to do the hard labor in post-slavery Latin America. Not surprisingly, Hindu Indians brought along their vibrant Holi tradition, which has colored the springs of Guyana, Suriname, and Trinidad and Tobago, ever since. In some parts of Latin America, Holi celebrations embrace all cultures in a particular region, and non-Hindus are more than happy to share in the good times.

Today approximately 70 to 80 percent of Latin Americans identify themselves as Catholic, and Latin America is the home of almost half of the world's Catholic population—around half a billion people. While this is a huge number and percentage, in recent years many Protestant Christian groups have gained membership throughout Latin America. Chile and Brazil have growing Protestant communities, and in Guatemala, Protestants make up a full 20 percent of the population. A growing branch of Protestantism in Latin America in recent years has been the Pentecostal Church, which proclaims the Bible as the literal word of God and that a direct relationship with him through acceptance of Jesus is the only way to enter heaven. Pentecostals share much in common with other evangelical faiths, including the belief that serving God requires converting others to Christianity.

Special Easter Foods in the Caribbean

Jamaicans feast on an Easter treat called *bulla*, a round cake eaten with avocado. Other traditional Jamaican Easter foods include plantain tarts, banana bread, bread pudding, and sweet potato pudding. Martiniquais of Martinique (a French Island in the Caribbean) prepare a special Easter dish of crab mixed with rice called *matoutou*.

In many parts of Latin America Easter is a sacred holiday that does not involve dyeing eggs or eating candy. But in other places, candy is a focus, and chocolate eggs make their appearance in stores many weeks ahead. On Easter, people exchange chocolate bunnies and large chocolate eggs, sometimes filled with hard candy or bon bons, and wrapped extravagantly in colored foils. Wealthy Brazilians might spend more than $100 on a chocolate egg for the special people in their lives.

Throughout the region Holy Week, or Santa Semana, is celebrated in full, marked by public performances and passion plays. In the lead-up to Easter, businesses and schools are closed all over Latin America.

A cardinal blesses worshippers during Easter Sunday Mass in Bogotá, Colombia.

Passover in Argentina

The largest population of Jews in Latin America lives in the city of Buenos Aires. In fact, Argentina is home to more than 200,000 Jews, which is the seventh-largest Jewish population in the world. The earliest Jewish settlers to Argentina were farmers who lived in agricultural colonies. Over the years, many Argentine Jews moved from farming to cattle ranching, a huge industry in a country that is famous for its beef around the world.

Despite living on a continent that is overwhelmingly Catholic, Argentine Jews have held fast to Passover traditions. In Argentina just as in every place where Jews live, Passover means cleaning the house of *chametz*, coming together as a family for the seder meal, reading the Haggadah and teaching the youngest family members about the Jewish Exodus from Egypt, and the ritual of the Passover meal.

Passover also means wonderful foods such as gefilte fish with horseradish, matzo ball soup, and roasted chicken. In Argentina pre-made Passover foods such as matzo ball mixes and unleavened bread have only recently been widely available in stores. As a result, Jewish families have traditionally prepared the holiday meal together at home from scratch.

Easter in the Bahamas

Easter in the Bahamas is a joyous time, in part influenced by British customs dating back to colonial times. Worship services begin before dawn, marking the end of the Easter Vigil that began on Holy Saturday. There are parades and feasts to mark this special day, and young girls and women wear colorful Easter bonnets decorated with ribbons, stencil drawings, paints, flowers, dried flowers, and other decorative materials. The day after Easter is known as Easter Monday and the first day of Bright Week. People enjoy feasts and parades and indulge in traditional

Eggs and Bread

Egg-rolling competitions are popular among children in the Bahamas, as they are on other Caribbean islands with British influence. Caribbean Christians also prepare hot cross buns, the European bread that symbolizes the death and Resurrection of Jesus.

activities: Catholics and Anglicans douse each other with the perfumed holy water that they received on Easter for use at home. Egg-rolling competitions are also popular for children.

Holi in the Caribbean

During the late 1800s, the British, who had colonized parts of the Caribbean and northern South America, brought indentured servants from India to harvest sugarcane and other crops, replacing the African slaves who had been freed. Today, Guyana in South America is about 35 percent Hindu and Suriname and the islands of Trinidad and Tobago are both more than 20 percent Hindu. Though they may never have set foot in India, these Caribbean Hindus know how to throw a raucous and all-embracing Holi celebration.

As in many parts of the world, Holi lasts for two days in the Caribbean. On the night of the full Moon before Holi, Hindus of Guyana, Suriname, and Trinidad and Tobago gather around a huge bonfire just as their fellow believers do in other parts of the world.

Surinamese Hindus stand around the bonfire that marks the first day of the Holi spring festival. Bonfires that signify the burning of the demoness Holika are attended by many of Suriname's large Hindu-origin population, and are followed by the spring festival of colors.

In Guyana, Hindus also invite non-Hindu Guyanese to join in the festivities and initiate them by covering them with colored powder. Music is an integral part of the celebrations. Guyana's Hindus dance to traditional Indian music played on a wide variety of musical instruments, such as the *dholak* (drum) and *jhaals* (little finger cymbals). In Suriname, Hindus wish each other "Holi Mubarak" ("Happy Holi") and throw colored powder, water, and water balloons on each other. They distribute sweets among their neighbors on this day and sing traditional songs. As in Guyana, non-Hindus also join in the celebrations. In Trinidad and Tobago, Holi includes various sports events and contests such as flag-grabbing and eating *roti* (a flat unleavened Indian bread).

The joy of Holi is that it seems to dissolve old disputes and animosities between community members, young and old alike, if only for one day. In these small Caribbean countries, people of all faiths live together in a relatively small space. It is not uncommon to see many non-Hindus participating in Holi celebrations, be they Christian or Muslim. In fact, in Guyana, some Muslim and Hindu religious observances are public holidays—including the Muslim Eid al-Adha, Eid al-Fitr, and Mouloud, and the Hindu celebrations of Diwali and Holi—although both are minority religions.

Proximity between people of different faiths and the national recognition of important holidays provide opportunities to learn about and share cultures and traditions with people of other groups and faiths. While relations are not always harmonious, the people of

Hindu children in Trinidad take part in the celebration of Holi, a national celebration in Trinidad where people from all walks of life join in the fun of the spraying of *abeer* (colored liquid) and dancing.

Sending Prayers Skyward

In Grenada, Trinidad and Tobago, and Guyana, Easter Monday brings remarkable kite-flying competitions, with prizes awarded for the best kites. For some, the kite flying symbolizes the Resurrection of Jesus. In Guyana, kite flyers often tie wishes or prayers to their kites. As the kites fly higher, their strings are cut in the hope that the kites will carry their messages to God.

the Caribbean take pride in their festivals. There is even a saying among Hindus during Holi: "Do not be angry, it is Holi."

Easter in Grenada

Easter in Grenada is marked by prayer services held early in the morning. During the Easter weekend the old and young alike take part in flying kites, which come in many shapes, sizes and colors. In addition, the Easter holiday signals the beginning of the season when Grenadians picnic at the beaches, watching regattas (boat races). In Grenada these races are collectively called the Grenada Round-the-Island Easter Regatta and include short races as well as the well-known race around the islands.

Vivid Easter Processions in Guatemala

On Easter in Guatemala worship services begin quite early in the morning. Guatemalans celebrate the day by wearing the traditional Mayan attire and participating in processions through the streets carrying statues of Jesus. In certain regions of Guatemala, such as in the city of Antigua, Easter celebrations are known for their elaborate and beautiful processions that are attended by thousands of locals as well as tourists from all over the world. Along cobblestone streets, intricately designed carpets made of colored sawdust and other natural materials are laid down. Later a solemn procession of actors playing Roman centurions, or soldiers, marches over the carpets, carrying a statue of Jesus hanging on the cross. The delicate sawdust carpets are kicked up as the procession passes over them and are destroyed, not to be seen again until the next Easter.

A Mayan Spring Observance in Mexico

Since ancient times the Maya have celebrated the spring equinox by gathering at the ancient city of Chichén Itzá, constructed more than 2,500 years ago. Created with materials from the surrounding jungle in the southeastern Mexican region of the Yucatán, and without the aid of the wheel or metal tools, Chichén Itzá is an incredible assembly of buildings and pyramids that demonstrates the sophistication of the ancient Mayan society.

The Maya are known for their remarkable achievements in mathematics (they invented the concept of zero well before Western civilizations) and astronomy. They developed a sophisticated calendar that accurately tracks the changing seasons. In fact, the pyramid of El Castillo (the castle) at Chichén Itzá was built to be aligned with the Sun and work as a massive sundial to accurately show the spring equinox and the autumn solstice. Since the Maya planned their lives and planting times (especially the planting and harvesting of corn) around the seasons, this gigantic sundial was essential to their survival.

In ancient times on the morning of the spring equinox, the Maya would gather to watch the Sun form triangles on the top of one side of El Castillo. These triangles would appear in greater numbers throughout the day and then work their way down the pyramid like a gigantic sunlit snake. The snake was known to the Maya as Kukulkan, or feathered serpent, and El Castillo also goes by the name Kukulkan. At the base of the pyramid, the Maya carved heads of the feathered serpent and one of them is illuminated by the end of the snake's descent on the spring equinox.

Mighty Mayan Achievements

The Maya are believed to have originated in the Yucatán around 2600 B.C.E. and then spread to present-day southern Mexico, northern Belize, Guatemala, and Honduras. In addition to being known for their astronomy, mathematics, and pyramids, they also developed a form of hieroglyphic writing (symbols or pictures that represent concepts, things, or sounds). This hieroglyphic system helps researchers today to better understand this rich and remarkable culture.

The massive 75-foot high stone pyramid, El Castillo, at the ancient city of Chichén Itzá, Mexico. The staircase railings of El Castillo were carved with feathered serpents in such a way that the snakes seem to travel down the steps to the plaza with the movement of the Sun.

For the Maya, the descent of the snake in the form of sunlit triangles symbolized the delivery of prosperity from the heavens to the people. It told them when to start planting the crops in the spring. In the fall, the sun snake started at the base of El Castillo and slithered back up the pyramid, signifying the autumn equinox, or time to harvest the crops.

The Mayan cities were abandoned for hundreds of years even before the arrival of the Spaniards, and many were destroyed after the Spanish colonized Latin America. Nevertheless, in recent years the ancient spring equinox observance has been revived, bringing thousands—including the ancestors of the ancient Mayans and tourists alike—to Chichén Itzá and El Castillo to watch the snake's descent.

The Firing of the Judases on Easter Sunday in Mexico

The Firing of the Judases in San Miguel de Allende—also home to a devout passion play—is an Easter tradition that has grown so popular with tourists that it is now sponsored by hotels and other businesses.

Two women pray during Easter services in the Metropolitan Cathedral in Mexico City, Mexico.

At 1:00 P.M., after church on Easter, in a central garden in the city, huge papier-mâché replicas of unpopular people—former presidents, politicians, and of course, Judas Iscariot—hang from ropes that are extended from trees to buildings around the plaza. The oversized puppets have firecrackers tied around their waists.

At the designated hour, all the fireworks are set off in a series of enormous explosions, after which paper arms, legs, torsos, and hands float to the ground. Although often only the head remains dangling from the rope, the event is not as morbid, as it might sound. It is festive and fun, especially for the kids, who grab the blown off papier-mâché body parts and duel with other armed children. Sometimes the lonely heads are taken down and sold to tourists.

Easter Festivities in Uruguay

Uruguayans enjoy a weeklong holiday throughout Holy Week. In parts of the country the week is also celebrated as La Semana Criolla, or "Rodeo Week." Gauchos (Uruguayan cowboys) entertain the crowds with their stunts and horseback-riding skills. On Easter day itself, Uruguayans visit their friends and family members and exchange greetings.

Middle East

Though most countries in the Middle East are predominantly Muslim, the biggest spring festivals in this part of the world are Navruz, celebrated by Persians in Iran; and Passover celebrated by the Jews of Israel. Although many Persian Muslims celebrate Navruz, it is not originally a Muslim holiday. Around the time when their neighbors are celebrating Navruz, Jews are observing Passover. In Israel, the official Jewish state established after World War II, Jews make up close to 77 percent of the population.

Navruz in Iran

On the Wednesday evening before Navruz begins, many Iranians observe a custom that has been compared to Halloween. On this night, bonfires are lit in the streets and people jump over them as a way of celebrating the end of the old year and any bad luck associated with it. Because it is believed that spirits of dead ancestors come out on this night, children dress up, covering their heads as if in mourning. The children go to their

Iraqi Kurdish women and children dance during Navruz celebrations in northern Iraq. Navruz, an ancient Persian festival, is celebrated on the first day of spring in countries including Iraq, Turkey, Afghanistan, and Iran. The festival is mainly a Kurdish event in Iraq and Turkey.

Children receive sweets for Navruz at the Zoroastrian temple in Chakchak, Iran.

neighbors' houses, banging on pots with spoons in the hope of getting sweets and dried fruit.

Perhaps the most important part of the New Year ritual is setting the Haft Seen with seven items. In addition, today in Iran many Haft Seen tables include an Iranian book called *Shahnameh* (The epic of kings) rather than the Quran, the holy book of Muslims. The *Shahnameh* is the national epic poem of the Persian world written by Persian poet Ferdowsi around 1000 C.E. It relates the real and mythic past of Iran from the time of the creation of the world up until the Islamic conquest of Iran in the seventh century. Some Iranians feel that the *Shahnameh* is more suitable on the Haft Seen because it is a reflection of Persian values and identity.

On the night before the new year, most Iranians prepare and cook a special dish of fried fish and herbed rice. Often a baked egg dish that contains an assortment of fresh herbs called *koukou sabzi* is also served. The next day, the traditional food will be rice and noodles.

In modern Iran, Navruz lasts for 13 days. The exact second that Navruz begins is called "Saal Tahvil." After the Saal Tahvil, people hug and kiss and exchange happy new year greetings and presents. Traditional gifts include gold coins. Children also receive special presents and sweet treats such as *aajil*, a mixture of nuts with raisins and other dried fruit.

The first days of this 13-day observance are spent visiting older family members, as well as friends and other relatives. On the 13th day, everyone in Iran goes outdoors and heads to parks for a picnic. This day in nature is called *Seezdeh be dar* (which means "getting rid of the omen of the 13th day," or "to avoid bad luck on this day"). While

A Change for the Table

Wine was once a traditional part of Navruz, but it no longer is in Muslim countries where alcohol is prohibited. Wine has been replaced by vinegar on the Haft Seen table.

An Iranian boy buys a decorative painted egg, a symbol of the Iranian new year, Navruz, in a market. The new solar year begins for Zoroastrians on the first day of spring, March 21.

picnicking, some Iranians also dance, listen to music, and take part in sporting events and other games. It is also customary for young women who hope to be married to go into a field and tie shoots from young plants into a knot, as a symbol of the marriage knot.

Kosher for Passover in Israel

In Israel both secular and observant Jews celebrate Passover, and signs of the holiday appear throughout the country weeks ahead. It is easy to find Passover foods in the stores. Chocolate chips, cheese, and jams are labeled "Kosher for Passover" so that shoppers know that there are no forbidden ingredients. Even sugar, which often contains cornstarch, has a substitute corn-free kosher version. In addition to the stores, at the snack stands in public parks, kids are relieved to see that they can eat the ice cream, clearly marked "Kosher for Passover."

As Israel is a relatively new country, many people who live there still feel closely tied to the countries their families came from. The traditions

Shifting Jewish Population

More than 70,000 Jews living in Morocco immigrated to Israel after it became a Jewish state. Today only 5,000 Jews live in Morocco.

Ultra-Orthodox Jewish Hasidic children burn *chametz* in the Mea Shearim neighborhood of Jerusalem prior to the start of the Passover holiday. Passover is a time when religious Jews thoroughly clean their homes and refrain from eating leavened bread.

of these many other countries shape Passover in Israel. For example, Jews from Iran pass around scallions during seder. While reciting a Passover song about God rescuing the Jews from Egypt, they lightly tap the scallions on the shoulder of the person on their right. This custom reminds Jews that their ancestors were slaves who were sometimes beaten.

Moroccan Jews living in Israel also have a special tradition, called Mimouna, that ends the seven days of Passover. In the days following the seder, Moroccan Jews make a variety of sweets—egg white cookies, coconut cakes with almond and chocolate, candied and dried fruits, jellies, and the almond paste marzipan. At the hour that Passover ends, Moroccan Jews set the Mimouna table and put out all the sweets. Then they place

The Growing Kibbutz Movement

The kibbutz was first established in the early 20th century, well before the Israeli State was formed. These communal farms grew the fruits and vegetables for which Israel is now well known. Today there are more than 250 kibbutzim in Israel and 100,000 members live there.

a fish—a fertility symbol—on a table outside their homes. Guests arrive and sample the sweets and then move on to the next home where more Mimouna treats are offered.

More than 100,000 of the people living in Israel live in kibbutzim, communal farms whose residents work together to provide the community with food, clothing, a place to live, and medical services. A kibbutz seder might have a children's choir to sing the songs and many members to lead the seder. The kibbutz movement also created its own Haggadah—the Jewish collection of prayers and stories that tell the Exodus story—with some unique elements, including a special prayer to honor springtime.

North America

Spring celebrations are popular across North America in March and April and include Easter, Passover, Holi, and Navruz. North America is a continent of immigrants from every corner of the world. The people of the United States and Canada pride themselves on the fact that their political history emphasizes freedom of expression and freedom of religion. At any given time during the springtime, there are celebrations and spring rites representing countless faiths and cultures. Still, North America is largely a Christian continent, and Easter, the holiday celebrating the Resurrection of Jesus Christ, is its most widespread spring celebration.

Easter in North America

While the United States and Canada are not officially Christian, Good Friday in Canada is a national holiday, and in the United States the president recognizes Easter by sponsoring events such as the annual White House Egg Roll.

The focus on Christianity is not surprising given that it is practiced by close to 66 percent of all Canadians and 76 percent of Americans. Within the United States and Canada hundreds of Christian denominations exist, including many branches of Protestantism and Catholicism. Even people who do not practice any Christian faith may participate in some secular Easter traditions, such as dyeing eggs and eating chocolate.

Revelers with colorful hats take part in the annual Easter Day Parade along Fifth Avenue in New York City.

Good Friday's Name

The original name of Good Friday may have been God's Friday because in Early Modern English, *good* meant "holy." Also, the two words were often interchangeable as in, "God be with you," now evolved to "good-bye."

Passover in North America

For Jewish communities throughout North America and the world, Passover commemorates the Exodus of the Jews from slavery in Egypt around 1200 B.C.E. The highlight of Passover is the observance of the seder at which the guests eat special kinds of food, listen to narratives about the Exodus from Egypt and freedom from slavery, sing songs, and offer special prayers.

The United States and Canada are home to large Jewish communities from many parts of the world, including the former Soviet Union, Germany, the Middle East, and Israel. These Jewish immigrants have helped shape holiday traditions in North America.

Social change in North America has also affected this holiday tradition. As people in North America have grown more sensitive to the issue of equality between men and women, versions of the Haggadah have been developed that use gender-neutral words to describe God, and include mention of some of the important Jewish

Three children raise their glasses filled with grape juice in place of wine during a seder celebrating Passover at a synagogue in Cedar Rapids, Iowa.

women throughout history. However, despite these changes, the Passover seder is easily recognizable whether one is in an Orthodox home or the home of Jews who follow a progressive approach to Judaism.

Growing Immigrant Groups Bring Their Spring Traditions

Spring festivals have been brought to North America by immigrants from all over the world. Latino Easter traditions such as Holy Week festivities are common in areas where there are immigrants from Latin America and the Caribbean, as well as in the southwest regions of the United States that were once part of Mexico. In communities such as New York City, where there are many Hindus, especially immigrants from India, Guyana, and Trinidad, Holi is celebrated in lavish style.

A traditional Haft Seen table celebrating Navruz, the Persian New Year, is seen set in the State Dining Room of the White House in Washington, D.C. The Haft Seen table displays items symbolizing new life (wheat sprouts growing in a pot), love (dried fruit of the oleaster tree), beauty and health (apples), sunrise (sumac berries), prosperity (coins), patience (vinegar), affluence (a sweet pudding), and medicine (garlic).

Zoroastrians and Persians from Iran (and other countries influenced by Persia throughout early history) have also brought with them their Navruz customs and rites. Followers of the Baha'i Faith number close to 120,000 in the United States and 30,000 in Canada. Their celebrations of Naw Rúz (as they call Navruz) often show a mixture of tradition combined with inventiveness. For example, in Washington, D.C., one group of Baha'i might celebrate with a luncheon cruise on the Potomac, whereas Baha'i members in Florida may have a big Persian dinner followed by dancing to music provided by a D.J. Some communities like to have a Persian member of the faith talk about the meaning of the holiday based on ancient times. Because the belief that all humanity belongs to one family is central to Baha'i religion, their focus is on getting together as a community rather than on specific individual practices.

Easter in Canada

French explorers and colonists first brought Roman Catholicism to Canada. While the Protestant English eventually won control, Roman Catholicism has continued to dominate, especially in French-speaking areas of the country. Today the percentage of Roman Catholics in Canada is around 45 percent and only 23 percent identify themselves as Protestant. There

Record-Setting Egg

Canada has something no other country can claim—the world's largest Easter egg! Located in Vegreville, Alberta, Canada, this massive 5,000-pound egg was created in 1975 to honor early Ukrainian settlements in an area east of Edmonton, Alberta, Canada. Made of aluminum, it is more than 18 feet long and features 524 star patterns and more than 2,000 triangular pieces, and it turns like a weathervane. Designed by computer scientist Ronald Resch, this elegant egg took 12,000 hours of labor to complete and is recognized globally as an artistic masterpiece, as well as the first computer modeling of an egg. Thousands of tourists travel to Vegreville every year just to gaze at this enormous oval in the sky.

A priest blesses the traditional Easter baskets of three siblings at a Ukrainian Catholic Church in Ontario, Canada.

are also approximately 400,000 Canadians who are members of the Eastern Orthodox Church.

In Canada, Good Friday is a national holiday. On this day, Christians may attend a special service mourning the death of Jesus. This service often lasts from noon until 3 P.M., representing the last three hours of darkness that Jesus suffered on the cross. Some Christians fast on this day. When they eat, it is generally fish instead of meat.

Today, there are approximately 1 million Canadians of Ukrainian descent. Canada and the Ukraine remain close friends, and Canada was the first country in the West to recognize the Ukraine's independence from the Soviet Union in 1991. On Easter morning, Orthodox Ukrainians bring their Easter baskets to church to receive the priest's blessing. The baskets are heaped full of colored eggs, ham, beets with horseradish, Easter bread called *paska*, and cottage cheese. These foods are then eaten for Easter breakfast, beginning always with the colored eggs.

For the Ukrainians in Canada, eggs have another meaning. Craftspeople decorate eggs in an elaborate process called *pysanky* that is believed to transfer goodness from the household to the designs on the eggs, and thus to protect the family and home from misfortune. Spirals and other designs painted on the eggs are believed to trap evil, just as a spider traps a fly in the latticework of its web. Because of the meaning attached to the eggs, *pysanky* are distributed in a variety of ways: three or four might be placed on family graves, a couple go to the local priest, and in rural areas, several may be put

Precious Eggs

To understand how precious *pysanky* are to the Canadians of Ukrainian descent, one has only to visit the Ukraine Museum in Saskatoon, in the Canadian province of Saskatchewan. There visitors will find, in addition to all the artifacts that represent Ukrainian history in Canada, *pysanky* that are more than 100 years old, brought to the country by early immigrants.

under hens' nests to encourage good laying or under the beehive to ensure a plentiful production of honey.

As is true for Christians around the world, eggs, historically forbidden during Lent, are a treat during Easter. In parts of Quebec they are served with maple syrup, one of Canada's specialties. As in the United States, Canadian children also celebrate Easter with egg hunts in family yards and at local parks or church grounds. Because in Canada (and in northern parts of the United States) one cannot always count on having spring flowers and grass poking through the ground at Easter time, parents sometimes find themselves hiding chocolate and candy-filled eggs in snow banks.

Avian Flu and the Egg Hunt

In recent years, bird flu, a virulent disease that can spread from animals to humans, hit poultry farms hard throughout Asia and spread to other countries, including Canada. Because it is such a deadly strain that still does not have an effective treatment, some Canadian Easter egg hunts have had to be canceled. In North America, there has not been widespread human illness or death associated with the bird flu, and the egg will most likely remain part of Easter for years to come.

Passover in Canada

Around 350,000 Jews live in Canada. Many Jews came to Canada in the 1880s to escape the pogroms (government-led campaigns of persecution) of eastern Europe and in the early 20th century to flee World War I and World War II and the Holocaust. Having fled religious oppression in their homelands, these Jews were often determined to express their faith and culture in Canada. Canada's Passover, then, reveals strong strains of Passover as it was celebrated in Europe.

Although Canada has a large Jewish population, kosher Passover foods are hard to come by in many Canadian stores. In cities with strong Jewish communities, such as Toronto and Montreal, kosher foods are available but expensive. And in smaller communities, they are not available at all. Canadian Jews have to be resourceful, checking labels carefully to avoid *chametz* (and, for Ashkenazi Jews, *kitniyot* as well) or preparing Passover foods from scratch.

In Canada Passover is not a national holiday and schools are in session. While Canada is religiously tolerant by law, Jewish Canadians must request leave if they wish to take time off during Passover.

Holi Can Be Frosty in Canada

More than 150,000 Canadians claim Hinduism as their religion. They or their ancestors come from all over the world—including East Africa, South Africa, Fiji, Mauritius, Guyana, Trinidad, India, Singapore, and Malaysia—and they often observe some of the traditions of their homelands.

Fun without Freezing

A few determined Canadian Hindus refused to give up the water tradition of the holiday. In 2000 at York University in Ontario, a group of Hindu friends began an annual tradition of playing Holi outdoors regardless of the weather. In order to lessen the impact of being splashed with icy water on a cold Canadian day, they fill water bottles with hot water and stay close to sheltered areas of campus.

Because it is often still quite cold in Canada when Holi comes, Hindus there tend to celebrate indoors, often renting large halls for their gatherings. Some traditions must be adapted to the indoor setting. For example, Canadian Hindus still douse one another with colorful powder, but they leave out the water that would create a mess. Even so, they sometimes have to pay extra cleanup fees!

Persians of All Faiths Celebrate Navruz in Canada

More than 120,000 people of Iranian ancestry live in Canada, largely in urban areas, including Toronto, Vancouver, and Montreal. Recently the Canadian province of British Columbia officially recognized Navruz, or Norouz (as it is often spelled throughout the world). March 21 in British Columbia is now called Norouz, much to the delight of the thousands of Iranians who live there. All over Canada where Persians live, Navruz is celebrated in homes and community centers.

All Navruz celebrations include the traditional Haft Seen table, and many Persian celebrants wear traditional Iranian clothing and share dances with the many children. In order to attend some Navruz celebrations, families must purchase tickets. Other communities also have parades during Navruz and invite talented Persian musicians and dancers to participate.

The Spring Is Celebrated by Indigenous Canadians

The Inuit are the largest group of indigenous people in Canada. More than 55,000 Inuit live in the country's far north across 53 towns. In early April in the town of Iqualit the Inuit celebrate, and invite others to celebrate, Toonik Tyme. This spring festival began in 1964 as a way to unwind at the end of winter, as well as to attract tourism and to share Inuit traditions with non-Inuit people from Canada and beyond. The weeklong festival features events including seal hunting and skinning, harpoon throwing, igloo building, ice sculpture contests, dog team races, and a fishing derby (the first person to catch a fish wins). As is clear from the featured events, it may be spring in northern Canada, but it is usually still very cold, with temperatures averaging around 6 degrees Fahrenheit.

An Inuit man works on a traditional igloo in preparation for the celebrations of Toonik Tyme in the Canadian Arctic community of Iqualit.

Newer additions to the schedule include Toonik Tyme Fear Factor, a fashion parade and show, a craft fair, and scavenger hunts. The Fear Factor contest is similar to the television show by the same name, which means that the lucky contestants get to eat squirmy maggots and jump from dizzying heights. The prize for winning this contest is 5,000 Canadian dollars.

Easter in the United States

In the United States, Roman Catholics make up close to a quarter of all Christians, and Protestant denominations make up 52 percent. In addition, around 3 million people are members of Eastern Orthodox churches. The Easter Bunny hopped its way into American Easter celebrations in the 18th century. The German custom of receiving a basket filled with candy by an Easter bunny came with European immigrants to Pennsylvania Dutch country, where it caught on. Children (good children anyway) woke

When Christians Do Not Celebrate Easter

Some Christian denominations such as Jehovah's Witnesses and the United Church of God do not celebrate Easter or Christmas because of the pagan roots of these holidays. Because Christmas and Easter do not appear in the Bible, Christians who follow it literally do not observe these holidays.

Children run with their baskets into a field covered with colored eggs during an annual Easter egg hunt in Ohio.

on Easter to find colored eggs and other treats in a basket (the rabbit's nest). Today, the bunny still delivers. As in some parts of Europe, families in the United States paint Easter eggs together at home and participate in Easter egg hunts.

Many Protestants begin their celebration on Easter at a sunrise service in the United States. This tradition may have its roots in the Bible books of John, Matthew and Luke, which suggest that Jesus' Resurrection happened before dawn. Ancient traditions might also have contributed to the ritual of the sunrise service, because many ancient cultures had spring rituals of building bonfires at dawn to symbolize the triumph of light and life over death and darkness. Whatever its true origins, the sunrise Easter service is one of great joy as the Sun comes up and overtakes the darkness of the night.

Sunrise Services in California

Sunrise Easter services are held throughout the United States at churches as well as outdoor locations such as parks and cemeteries, where the sunrise can be seen easily. Each year, Arlington National Cemetery and the Washington Memorial in Washington, D.C., hold large outdoor services. A nondenominational sunrise service is held each Easter at the

A Classic Setting for Spring

During the Hollywood Bowl nondenominational sunrise service on Easter, a large youth chorus wearing black robes is seated in a Latin cross formation. After a signal from the orchestra conductor, the children stand up and remove their robes, displaying white vestments and forming an enormous living cross.

Hollywood Bowl in California, in a tradition that began in 1921. In 2007 the Hollywood Bowl celebrated its 86th anniversary, with the Los Angeles Philharmonic Orchestra playing as the Sun peeked over the nearby hills and the audience sang the Psalm of Praise.

The Easter Parade in New York City

In many American churches, Easter is a time to wear one's finest clothing and hats. The women's fancy hats, or Easter "bonnets," are usually light-colored with a wide brim, decorated with ribbons, flowers, or other

spring colors and themes. Easter hats gained even more popularity after the Irving Berlin song "Easter Parade" became famous in 1948. The song was featured in a film with the same title that starred two mega-stars of the time, Judy Garland and Fred Astaire.

From around the turn of the 19th century to the 20th, Americans often stretched their legs after church on Easter (and showed off their fine new clothes) by taking a walk around the town. These casual strolls may have eventually grown into the Easter parades that are now popular all over the United States. The grandest and most famous Easter Parade, the one that Berlin mentions in his celebrated song, is the annual parade in New York City along Fifth Avenue.

Two girls wearing specially decorated hats pass by St. Patrick's Cathedral during the Easter Day Parade along Fifth Avenue in Manhattan, New York City.

During the middle of the 19th century the upper class in New York City would parade in their new frocks and dress clothes after attending one of the Easter services at a Fifth Avenue church. Today, the parade is an extravaganza of outrageous outfits—from bonnets made of real flowers with live birds' nests in them, to high-fashion pets with their equally high-couture owners. Some simply choose to wear traditional Easter clothes. The parade is not highly organized and does not have floats or marching bands, but it is definitely the place to be in New York City on Easter Day.

A Sunrise Service in the Moravian Church in Bethlehem, Pennsylvania

Since the late 18th century, members of the Moravian Church have cleaned the gravestones of their ancestors and loved ones in the Moravian cemeteries (usually referred to as God's Acre), as a way of preparing for Easter. Families and church groups clean and decorate gravestones with flowers, turning the cemetery into a colorful, lovely place. Then, on Easter Sunday, members of Moravian Easter bands call congregants to the God's Acre Sunrise Service by playing music to rouse them from their sleep. Bethlehem, Pennsylvania, is known for its trombone choir that calls the congregation to their sunrise service in the old Moravian cemetery. The trombones play hymns throughout town before dawn on Easter Sunday and then continue their lively and joyous music at the cemetery as the Sun rises.

Good Friday in Providence, Rhode Island

For many Catholics of Latin American origin in the United States, Good Friday is an occasion for the processions and passion plays that are prevalent throughout Central and South America, as well as Spain and its other former colonies. In urban communities such as Providence, Rhode Island, with immigrants from Colombia, the Dominican Republic, and Mexico, as well as small New Mexican towns where Nuevos Mejicanos have lived for centuries, it is common to see parades through parts of towns on Good Friday. During these processions, church members reenact the last hours of Jesus' life. While Good Friday is not a national public holiday in the United States, in some states schools and businesses are closed.

The First White House Egg Roll

In 1878 President Rutherford B. Hayes's wife, Lucy, held the first public Easter egg roll on the lawn of the White House on Easter Monday, inviting all who wanted to participate. While sometimes canceled because of bad weather and during wartime, it is a tradition that continues to this day.

Egg Rolling on the White House Lawn in Washington, D.C.

Since President Rutherford B. Hayes's wife, Lucy, held the first public Easter egg roll on the lawn of the White House on Easter Monday in 1878, every Easter Monday, presidents and first ladies have welcomed the children onto the lawn. Children roll eggs across the lawn with spoons, not down a hill as is customary in Europe. Other activities include egg dyeing and decorating, and an egg hunt. Cabinet members and famous people such as musicians, movie stars, and the official White House Easter Bunny also come to spend time with the youngsters, some of them sharing their special talents. When the egg rolling is over,

Children roll Easter eggs during the annual White House Easter Egg Roll on the South Lawn of The White House, in Washington, D.C. The White House Easter Egg Roll has been an annual tradition since 1878, when it was started by President Rutherford B. Hayes's wife.

all participants leave with a special wooden egg that contains the signatures of the president and the first lady.

Today, to be admitted to the White House event, children must be between three and seven years old; they are issued free tickets on a first-come, first-served basis. In addition to the famous performers that attend every year, actors playing historical figures such as Lucy Hayes, Thomas Jefferson, Abraham Lincoln, and Betsy Ross wander the South Lawn entertaining the children. Some years the White House Easter egg collection is displayed. This collection is made up of eggs representing all 50 states and the District of Columbia, painted by talented local artists.

Passover Traditions in the United States

The United States has the second-largest population of Jews in the world, at more than 5 million. The number of Jews in the United States is just slightly smaller than in Israel today. Especially in large cities where an overwhelming majority of U.S. Jews live, strong support systems exist to help Jews

A father helps his seven-year-old son recite from the Haggadah during a seder in Queens, New York.

carry on their Passover traditions. Indeed, even among nonreligious Jews in the United States, Passover is widely celebrated as a way of passing cultural traditions on to the next generation. In the United States, Jews often invite non-Jewish friends to the Passover table to share in the celebration.

On college campuses close to Jewish communities, it is often possible to attend an Orthodox Hasidic Passover at Chabad Houses, which, according to the Chabad House of Greater Boston, are "dedicated to furthering the understanding and observance of Jewish traditions to all, regardless of their background." These houses provide a "home away from home" for Jewish students and young adults who live far from their families, as well as others within the communities. Hasidic rabbis live in or work with

The Hasidic Movement

The Hasidic branch of Judaism has its roots in the 18th-century attacks on Jewish communities in eastern Europe. While educated Jews found comfort in the holy books, poor and oppressed Jews who had lost everything in the violence started to practice a mystical Judaism under the guidance of a man given the title of the Baal Shem Tov, who had studied with a secret society of Jewish mystics. Instead of focusing on gaining knowledge, the Baal Shem Tov encouraged the poor to feel the power of God. Feeling emotionally uplifted in intense prayer and joyous singing was more important than knowing exactly what the words meant. Followers of the Baal Shem Tov. are called Hasidic Jews and at one time made up a large percentage—possibly even half—of all European Jews. The Hasidic leaders ensured that even poor and uneducated Jews could lead spiritual lives and feel part of the Jewish community. Today, Hasidic Jews still wear traditional clothing, often dark and conservative dresses for women and long dark coats for men. The men do not shave the hair on their faces, although they may shave their heads. Large communities of Hasidic Jews live in Israel, in a borough of Montreal called Outremont, and in New York City.

Reform Judaism

Reform Jews believe in a more modern view of Judaism and have embraced changes in some Jewish traditions, such as allowing the seating of men and women together in the synagogue or not following the kosher traditions for food preparation on a daily basis. Reform Judaism started in the Diaspora and today a majority of Jews in the United States practice Reform Judaism.

the houses, which can be found in Boston, Massachusetts; Los Angeles, California; Ann Arbor, Michigan; Amherst, Massachusetts; Hartford, Connecticut; Boca Raton, Florida, and many other communities.

Since Passover is a ritual feast, the same basic steps are followed at seders in New York, Chicago, or Los Angeles as in Jerusalem. But although the outline of the seder remains consistent across time and national borders, Jews are free to drop parts of the ceremony or add elements from other faiths (such as African-American spirituals or modern poetry) that make connections between the Israelites' bondage and the enslavement of other peoples.

However, because the seder is in a large part about ritual foods, even those American families who do not follow kosher customs throughout the year will often do so during Passover. Moreover, in the United States and especially in larger communities where Jews live—parts of New Jersey, California, and New York—kosher for Passover foods have been available in Jewish corner stores and major supermarkets alike for many years.

In recent years nontraditional seder offerings have begun to emerge. In 1993, the first feminist seder was held in New York City by Ma'yan, a women's project at the Jewish Community Center of Manhattan. This seder uses a specially written Haggadah that uses feminine language for God. During a feminist seder, a family's daughters, not the youngest son, as is traditional, ask the Four Questions that help tell the story of Passover. As Rabbi Joy Levitt of the Jewish Community Center explains in a PBS *Religion and Ethics NewsWeekly* broadcast, "A feminist Seder attempts to locate women in that story, not only the story of the liberation of the Israelites in Egypt but the continuing, evolving story of liberation of women everywhere."

Young Indian-Americans join in a mud sliding activity as part of the Holi festival of colors at a college in South Carolina.

Holi Parades and Parties across the United States

Approximately 1 million Hindus of Indian and Indo-Caribbean descent live in the United States, most in major urban centers on the East and West coasts. In New York City, Indians of Trinidadian and Guyanese descent celebrate the Caribbean version of Holi. The tradition began in 1990 in Queens with a large public parade including floats carrying beauty queen contest winners, prominent business people, politicians, and religious leaders. In a restriction unheard of in India, the colorful Holi dyes are not allowed along the parade route. Celebrants must hold their fire until they get to a community park at the end of the parade. There, children and adults alike douse one another with water and colored powder, or *abrac*. Even innocent bystanders are fair targets for kids firing super-soakers filled with purple dye.

Playing Holi on university campuses from California to Michigan brings together Indians from all over the world, some of whom are homesick for India or the Caribbean, or want to show their American-raised children what the festival is like. On campuses and at parades, many non-Hindus also participate in the fun, sometimes coming just to watch, only to find themselves drenched in a rainbow of colors.

Providing the Color for Holi

In India the special red and dark Holi dyes are called *gulal*. Hundreds of pounds of the pigments are imported from India for Holi celebrations in the United States, although at many events around the United States, non-permanent dyes have replaced the traditional permanent ones.

Persians of all Faiths Celebrate Navruz throughout the United States

Persians around the country celebrate Navruz by organizing fire jumps, parades, and parties. In New York City, a large parade features traditional Iranian dancing and elaborate floats. At universities around the country, Persian and Iranian students organize Navruz events. In Persian homes, as well as the homes of the Baha'is, the Haft Seen table will be prepared with the traditional objects, and might also include the holy books of many faiths—the Quran, Christian Bible, or writings of the Baha'i prophet Bahaullah.

On the West Coast, where many Iranians live, the Navruz New Year's countdown is shown on TV. Community centers play host to Iranians as well as non-Persian friends and neighbors who are along for the party. These community centers are important to the lives of Persians through-out the year, not just at Navruz. They also offer Farsi language classes and other cultural activities for children and adults and many welcome people of all backgrounds to participate in their unique and diverse culture.

Oceania

Oceania is an area in the Pacific Ocean that cradles the equator. Consisting of thousands of islands, the area is usually divided into three main regions: Polynesia, Micronesia, and Melanesia. The countries of Oceania include Australia, New Zealand, the Marshall Islands, Federated States of Micronesia, Papua New Guinea, Samoa, and Tonga. Almost all of Oceania is located in the Southern Hemisphere, which means that most "spring" celebrations of Easter and Holi actually happen in the Oceanian fall, when the weather is usually warm and dry (the coldest months are in June, July, and August).

In the 1800s Britain colonized many parts of Oceania, including New Zealand, Australia, parts of Micronesia, and Fiji, introducing Christianity to the indigenous people. By the 1970s Britain no longer held colonial power in this area, but many of the people still practiced Christianity. In Fiji, where the British had imported workers from India, a Hindu legacy remains. Today, more than 65 percent of Australians and more than 50 percent of New Zealanders practice some form of Christianity. In Fiji 50 percent are Christian and around 30 percent practice Hinduism.

Buns and Easter Bilbies in Australia

Easter is observed in Australia primarily by people of Anglo-Irish origin. They attend church services early in the morning and later have hot cross

buns for breakfast. Children receive chocolate eggs or eggs made of sugar that contain little toys. On Easter Sunday many families gather for a holiday meal, often roast lamb, beef, or chicken with roasted vegetables such as potatoes, carrots, and pumpkin, followed by an Easter egg hunt. In Australia, the traditional chocolate Easter bunny has been joined by a chocolate Easter bilby, an animal native to Australia that is now an

In Australia traditional chocolate Easter bunnies have been joined by chocolate Easter bilbies, like the one shown here. Bilbies, also known as rabbit-eared bandicoots, are an endangered species in Australia.

The Sensitive Bilby

Bilbies are also known as rabbit-eared bandicoots and are mostly found in the driest regions of interior Australia. With big ears, long hind legs, and bushy tails, the bilby can smell and hear very well, but has poor eyesight. For this reason, and because temperatures are cooler after sunset, bilbies mostly come out at night to eat. Their diet includes small insects such as termites and ants, seeds, fungi, and roots that they rake out of the sandy desert soil with their sharp claws and long tongues. The bilbies used to thrive in Australia but their population has dwindled. They must compete with rabbits for food, and foxes and feral cats hunt them. Droughts have killed some bilbies, as has poison meant to control the huge overpopulation of wild rabbits. Some of the land where bilbies used to live is now reserved for cattle and other livestock.

endangered species. Chocolate manufacturers contribute some of their bilby profits toward protecting the animal from extinction.

Easter Celebrations in Fiji

In Fiji, Good Friday is a day to mourn in church. During a somber service, Christians meditate on Jesus' suffering and death on the cross. On some islands Christians take part in Good Friday processions and reenactments of the Crucifixion. The main service on Good Friday takes place between midday and 3 P.M. In many churches, it takes the form of a meditation based on the few last words of Jesus on the cross, with hymns, prayers, and short sermons.

On Easter in Fiji the churches are decorated with flowers, and people sing hymns and special songs. The Monday after Easter is a national holiday with government offices, businesses, and schools closed for the day.

Holi Parties in Fiji

Holi is celebrated by Hindus to announce the arrival of spring. Because Fiji is in the Southern Hemisphere, it is fall—not spring—in March and April, but Hindus there celebrate nonetheless. Men go from house to house singing songs called *faag*. Families visit friends and relatives, exchange sweets, and douse one another with Holi colors. Non-Hindus and tourists to Fiji also sometimes join in the fun.

Easter at Community Halls in Kiribati

Kiribati is a country that is part of the region of Micronesia and straddles the equator. Since Kiribati is a Christian country (about 52 percent Roman Catholic, 40 percent Protestant), Easter assumes great importance there. On Easter Sunday the Kiribati attend a religious service and then a feast in the *maneaba* (community hall), where families perform local dances.

Easter Begins on Saturday in New Zealand

In New Zealand, Easter ceremonies begin on the night of Holy Saturday with an evening service. At church on Easter Sunday worshippers light large candles symbolizing hope and pass them from hand to hand. People also enjoy a special cake on Easter called *sinnel*, prepared with dried fruit and whisky or brandy. Because the Easter holiday lasts from Good Friday through the following Tuesday, New Zealanders often travel, spending Easter at their family homes or farms in the countryside.

Easter Is Both Sacred and Fun in Tonga

In Tonga, where the people are devout Christians, the festival of Easter assumes great importance. Apart from the traditional ceremonial prayers in churches, the people also organize a grand festival, complete with youth choirs, passion plays, concerts, and other cultural performances. Easter Monday is a public holiday, and Tongans take advantage of the long weekend to enjoy themselves with friends and family.

Glossary

abstinence   Self-restraint or self-denial of something, such as alcohol, for a period of time.

ancestor worship   Since pre-literate times, cultures have believed that there is life after death in some form. Communities provided food offerings to their deceased relatives and performed religious rites to keep their spirits pleased. In many parts of the world today, especially Africa, Asia, and Oceana, many still believe the dead have needs to be taken care of by the living and that there is a connection between the dead and the fertility of the land. To honor the connection, rites are performed especially during times of harvest and the festival associated with them.

animism   The belief that plants, trees, and other things in nature (the sky, mountains, rocks) have spirits or souls.

apostle   One chosen and trained by Jesus in the New Testament to preach the Gospel

archipelago   A chain or large group of islands in an ocean

Ascension Day   After Easter, the day of Jesus' Resurrection, comes Ascension Day, when Christians believe that Jesus rose from Earth into heaven.

Bible   Collection of religious writings used in both Judaism and Christianity.

colonial era   A period of time between the 17th to 19th century when many countries of the Americas and Africa were colonized by Europeans.

colonize   To travel to and settle in a foreign land that has already been settled by groups of people. To colonize can mean to take control of the indigenous groups already in the area or to wield power over them in order to control their human and physical resources.

deity   A god, goddess, or holy being

diaspora   This term refers to any geographic place where a group of people from a different culture settle that is not the country of origin of these people. For example, many Hindu Indians now live in the United States, a predominantly Christian country. The diaspora sometimes suggests the scattering of a group or culture that used to live together in one place. When referring to Jews, the Diaspora is capitalized.

equator   The imaginary line that extends around the Earth and that divides it into two halves. Each half is equal in distance from the north and south poles. The equator goes through the northern part of South America and central Africa.

fast   To abstain from eating for a set period of time, or to eat at only prescribed times of the day as directed by religious custom or law.

feast day   A day when a religious celebration occurs and an intricate feast is prepared and eaten.

gefilte fish   A food often served in shaped cakes or balls and often eaten during the Jewish celebration of Passover. This dish contains chopped fish with cracker crumbs, eggs, and spices.

imam   A Muslim ruler who claims religious privilege to serve as a leader based on his role as a successor to the Muslim prophet Muhammad.

indentured servants   An immigrant to the Americas or Australia between the 17th and 19th centuries who agreed to work for an employer for several years in exchange for his or her trip to the new country and for food and shelter.

Islam   The religion of Muslims throughout the world. This religion is based on the word of God that was revealed to the Muslim prophet Muhammad during the seventh century C.E. Islam also refers collectively to the people, culture, and countries where Muslims live.

Israelite   Someone who was part of the ancient group of Hebrew people that originally descended from Jacob, a biblical ancestor of the 12 tribes of Israel.

Kurds   A group, mostly Sunni Muslims, of the same ethnicity who live in Southwest Asia in an area that includes parts of Iraq, Iran, Armenia, Syria, and Turkey. Many Kurds would like their own homeland and have been persecuted by the countries in which they live.

legacy   Something that is passed down from a generation before. It can be something material such as an inheritance or a tradition or custom that is handed down through the generations.

liturgy   The kind of worship or service that is set forth by a religion. A liturgy can also refer to the specific way a Christian church (often Eastern Churches) celebrates Communion.

lore   The knowledge or wisdom that one has about traditions or customs that has been passed down through the generations, often through story telling.

monk   A holy man who removes himself from society to live in a religious community. There, he dedicates himself to a life or period of life of prayer, seclusion, and meditation.

monotheism   The belief in the supremacy of one god (and not many); Judaism, Islam, and Christianity are monotheist religions.

neo-pagan rites   Rituals practiced by adherents of modern paganism

observant Jews   A Jewish person who practices Judaism, the religion of the Jews. Observant Jews can be part of many kinds of Judaism, and not all observant Jews follow all of the Jewish traditions. However, observant Jews take part in the major traditions, holy days, and religious services associated with Judaism.

pagan   The original definition of *pagan* is someone in ancient Europe who lived in the countryside. Over time it has acquired a broader definition and refers to a person or group that does not believe in one god, but often believes in many gods that are closely connected to nature and the natural world.

passion play The reenactment, or retelling, of a central religious experience or event for a religious people. For example, the suffering and persecution of Jesus Christ that begins with the Last Supper and ends with his Crucifixion is often reenacted in passion plays before Easter.

Persian A person who comes from Iran or the language spoken by ancient Persians (also known as Farsi).

plague A disease that spreads widely and quickly through a community and often kills many people. A plague can also be a sudden eruption or emergence of something very horrible or disagreeable, such as a plague of locusts that destroys crops.

prophet An individual who acts as the interpreter or conveyer of the will of God and spreads the word to the followers or possible followers of a religion. A prophet can also be a stirring leader or teacher of a religious group. Capitalized it refers to Muhammad.

Psalms A biblical book of 150 hymns, poems, and songs of praise to God. Many psalms are credited to King David, the second of the Israelite kings, who created a united Israel and is known as the biblical slayer of the Philistine giant Goliath.

pyre A large file usually built with piles of wood on which the body of someone recently deceased is cremated in a religious ceremony.

reincarnation The belief in some religions that after a person or animal dies, his or her soul will be reborn in another person or animal; it literally means, "to be made flesh again." Many Indian religions such as Hinduism, Sikhism, and Jainism, believe in reincarnation.

secular Jews A person of Jewish descent who does not participate in the religious aspects of Judaism but often takes part in the rites, customs, and traditions celebrated by Jewish people worldwide.

shrine A place of prayer and worship that is connected to a holy person or an important religious event. A shrine can also be the burial place of a saint or other holy person.

sovereignty The right of a people, region, or a country to govern themselves without intervention or interference from outside political and cultural influences.

Bibliography

Anderson, Leona. *Vasantotsava: The Spring Festivals of India, Texts and Traditions.* New Delhi, India: D. K. Printworld, 1993.

Barnes, Trevor, ed. *The Kingfisher Book of Religions: Festivals, Ceremonies, and Beliefs from Around the World.* New York: Kingfisher Books, 1999.

Boyce, Mary. *Zoroastrians: Their Religions Beliefs and Practices.* Oxford, U.K.: Routledge, 2001.

Bradshaw, Paul, and Lawrence A. Hoffman, eds. *Passover and Easter: Origin and History to Modern Times.* Notre Dame, Ind.: University of Notre Dame Press, 2000.

Floyd, Pat. *Come to Easter: The Customs of the Lenten & Easter Seasons.* Nashville, Tenn.: Abingdon Press, 1999.

Johnson, Paul. *A History of Christianity.* New York: Atheneum, 1977.

Maier, Paul L. *In the Fullness of Time: A Historian Looks at Christmas, Easter, and the Early Church.* San Francisco: HarperSanFrancisco, 1991.

Nigosian, S. A. *The Zoroastrian Faith: Tradition and Modern Research.* Montreal, Quebec: McGill-Queen's University Press, 1993.

Robinson, George. *Essential Judaism: A Complete Guide to Beliefs, Customs, & Rituals.* New York: Simon & Schuster, 2001.

Shapiro, Edward S. *We Are Many: Reflections on American Jewish History and Identity.* Syracuse, N.Y.: Syracuse University Press, 2005.

Further Resources

∽

Books

Encyclopedia of World Religions. By Robert Ellwood and Gregory Alles, Eds. Published in 2007 by Facts On File, New York. A comprehensive encyclopedia of religious terms and religions, including ancient and indigenous religions, major world religions, and new religions.

Happy Nowruz: Cooking with Children to Celebrate the Persian New Year. By Najmieh Batmanglij. Published in 2008 by Mage Publishers, Washington, D.C. This photo-rich book is about more than just recipes. It is also a highly entertaining look at what is often referred to as Iran's happiest holiday. The first half of the book explains the many customs, stories, and preparations that lead up to Navruz, including Haji Firuz, planting the sprouts, egg decorating, the holiday table and the meaning of the seven items, just to name of few.

Handbook of Christian Feasts and Customs: the Year of the Lord in Liturgy and Folklore. By Frances Weiser. Published in 1952 by Harcourt, Brace and Company, New York. This book details a wide variety of Christian customs as well as the history and development of traditions and observances.

Hinduism. By Ranchor Prime. Published in 2005 by Firefly Books, Toronto. A colorful reference book for young adults that provides clear information about a complex religious belief system.

Holiday Symbols and Customs. By Sue Ellen Thompson. Published in 2003 by Omnigraphics, Detroit, Mich. Nearly 900 pages of information on religious and secular celebrations from around the world, including where and when the holiday is observed, lists of related symbols and traditions, as well as information on any closely related holidays.

Passover around the World. By Tami Lehman-Wilzig and illustrated by Elizabeth Wolf. Published in 2007 by Kar-Ben Publishing, Minneapolis, Minn. A book about Passover traditions that stem from the Jewish Diaspora. This colorful children's book includes sidebars explaining the history of how Jewish communities came to different parts of the world, as well as when and why many left for Israel in the 1940s and 1950s. Tasty Passover recipes accompany each entry divided by regional Passover traditions.

Seasons of Our Joy, a Modern Guide to the Jewish Holidays. By Arthur I. Waskow. Published in 1990 by Beacon Press, Boston. An interesting and innovative guide to the Jewish holidays, including age-old traditions, songs, recipes, and prayers. The author even suggests some new approaches to the holiday traditions, rites, and customs.

A World of Festivals: Holi–the Hindu Festival of Colours. By Dilip Kadodwala. Published in 2004 by Evans Brothers, London. This book describes how and why Holi is celebrated by taking the reader into the festival itself.

World Religions. By Warren Matthews. Published in 1991 by West Publishing Company, Minneapolis, Minn. Students will learn about the myriad diverse religious traditions around the world and learn how they have much in common in fundamental ways. The text combines with maps, photographs, timelines, and excerpts from holy books and texts.

Web Sites

About.com: Judaism. http://judaism.about.com/od/passover/Passover.htm. Good Web site with multiple links to terms and traditions related to Passover.

BBC.CO. UK. http://www.bbc.co.uk/religion/religions/christianity/holydays/easter.shtml. Web site and links from the British Broadcasting Company that includes a guide to Christian Easter as well as information on Christianity and its many beliefs, Holy Days, and subdivisions within Christianity.

Festival of Colors in India. http://www.thecolorsofindia.com/holi.html. A lively and informative set of pages on Holi history and celebration, this forms part of the much larger Colors of India cultural Web site.

Iranian New Year Norouz. http://www.persia.org/Culture/nowruz.html. Nice Web site that clearly and succinctly explains many aspects of this fascinating ancient observance. Also includes additional reading for those who want to dig deeper.

The Jewish Virtual Library. http://www.jewishvirtuallibrary.org/jsource/Judaism/holiday5.html. This online encyclopedia provides extensive and easy-to-follow explanations of practically every aspect of Judaism. Here, one can better understand all Jewish celebrations, as well as the history of Judaism, important Jewish women, the Holocaust, biographies of famous Jews in every field imaginable, and vital information on Israel.

National Geographic One Stop Research. http://www.nationalgeographic.com/onestop. Want to learn more about the countries of Asia, or view photographs from the Western Wall in Jerusalem? The one stop research Web site by National Geographic allows young teens to easily search for information on an endless array of topics, including spring festivals, and often provides links to photographs, art, games, videos, and lesson plans.

Virtual Jerusalem. http://www.virtualjerusalem.com/jewish_holidays/vjholidays.html. A fun site with terrific and extensive information on all of the Jewish holidays that take place throughout the year.

Picture Credits

PAGE

viii: AP Photo/Leslie Mazoch
3: AP Photo/Roland Weihrauch
7: AP Photo/Maxim Marmur
9: AP Photo/Daytona Beach News-Journal, Craig Litten
12: AP Photo/Bebeto Matthews
15: AP Photo/Dr. Scott M. Lieberman
16: Israel Sun/Landov
17: AP Photo/Richmond Times-Dispatch, P. Kevin Morley
20: AP Photo/Vahid Salemi
21: AP Photo/Murad Sezer
23: UPI Photo/Landov
25: AP Photo/Rajesh Kumar Singh
26: mundoview/Shutterstock
27: AP Photo/Shakil Adil
28: AP Photo/Rajesh Kumar Singh
30: AP Photo/Bikas Das
32: AP Photo/Denis Farrell
34: Reuters/Thierry Gouegnon/Landov
35: Reuters/Tara Todras-Whitehill/Landov
38: AP Photo/Schalk van Zuydam
41: AP Photo/M. Lakshman
42: Reuters/Shamil Zhumatov/Landov
45: Reuters/Kamal Kishore/Landov
47: AP Photo/Vincent Thian
48: Reuters/Vladimir Pirogov/Landov
50: AP Photo/Aaron Favila
52: Reuters/Ints Kalnins/Landov
54: Dimitar Bosakov/Shutterstock

56: UPI Photo/David Silpa/Landov
58: AP Photo/Srdjan Ilic
59: AP Photo/Alik Keplicz
61: Xinhua/Landov
62: NNS/Cleveland Plain Dealer/Landov
64: Chris Ratcliffe/Bloomberg News/Landov
65: AP Photo/Douglas Engle
67: AP Photo/Ricardo Mazalan
69: Reuters/Ranu Abelakh/Landov
70: AP Photo/Shirley Bahadur
73: Bufflerump/Shutterstock
74: AP Photo/Gregory Bull
75: AP Photo/Murad Sezer
76: AP Photo/Enric Marti
77: AP Photo/Vahid Salemi
78: Reuters/Gil Cohen Magen/Landov
80: Xinhua/Landov
81: AP Photo/The Gazette, Mark Christian
82: UPI Photo/Landov
84: AP Photo/Julie Jocsak,CP
88: AP Photo/Kevin Frayer,CP
89: AP Photo/Amy Sancetta
90: Xinhua/Landov
92: UPI Photo/Kevin Dietsch/Landov
93: AP Photo/Stuart Ramson
96: AP Photo/Independent-Mail, Ken Ruinard
98: Timothy Craig Lubcke/Shutterstock

Index

Page numbers in *italic* indicate illustrations.

A

5Afghanistan, 43–44
Africa, 32–40, *34*
Algeria, 33
ancestor worship, 38, 101
Andorra, 54
animism, 36, 101
apostle, 8, 101
archipelago, 39, 101
Argentina, 68
Ascension Day, 54, 101
Ashkenazi Jews, 17–18, 86
Asia, *41*, 41–51, *42*, *45*, *47*, *48*, *50*
Australia, *98*, 98–99
Avian flu, 86

B

Bahamas, 68–69
Belgrade, *58*
Bible, 6, 11, 24, 35, 39, 81, 89, 97, 101
bilbies, 98–99
bitter vegetable/herb, *15*, 16, 17
Bituun, 49
Brazil, *65*
Bulgaria, *54*, 54
Bwiti, 36–37

C

camel races, 33
Canada, 83–88, *84*, *88*
Caribbean. *See* Latin America
    and the Caribbean
Carnival, 5
Catholics, 38, 39, 44, 53, 64, 65, 66,
    80, 83, 88, 91. *See also* Easter
China, 44
chocolate, *34*, 35, 55, 56, 57, 58, 61,
    62, 67, 77, 78, 80, 85, 98–99
Choti Holi, 27
Christianity, 4, 5, 32, 34, 36,
    38, 63, 66, 80, 98

Colombia, *67*
colonial era, 32, 33, 101
colonization, 32, 38, 51, 65, 69, 73, 98, 101
Coptic Easter, 34–36
Côte d'Ivoire, *34*, 34–35
Cybele (fertility goddess), 4

D

Denmark, 55
diaspora, 28, 95, 101

E

Easter, 3–7, *9*, 9–10. *See also* Coptic Easter
    in the Bahamas, 68–69
    baskets, 10, 52, 58, 59, *84*, 84, *88*, 88
    in Belgrade, *58*
    bunnies, 3, 10, 52, 92, 92–93, 98
    in Canada, 83–85, *84*, *88*
    in China, 44
    Christian, 5
    in Côte d'Ivoire, *34*, 34–35
    eggs, 10, 23, 30, 35, 36, 46,
        51–63, *62*, 67, 80, *89*, 98
    in Egypt, 34–36
    in Fiji, 99
    in France, *56*, 56
    Granny, 58
    in Hungary, 56–57
    in Iceland, 57
    in Kazakhstan, 46–47
    in Kiribati, 100
    in Lithuania, 57
    in New Zealand, 100
    in North America, 10, *80*, 80
    in the Philippines, *50*, 50–51
    in South Africa, *32*, *38*, 38
    in Tonga, 100
    in Uganda, 39
    in Uruguay, 74
    in the United States, *2*, 88–93, *89*
Egypt, 34–36
Eostre (mother goddess), 3–4, 10

equator, 1, 98, 101
Ethiopia, 36
Europe, *52*, 52–64, *55*
Exodus, 11, 13, 14, 15, 68, 79, 81

F

Fallas Festival, *61*
fast, 7, 35–36, 47, 68, 84, 101
feast day, 4, 20, 102
Fiji, 99–100
Finland, 55–56
Firing of the Judases, 73–74
fortune telling, 28
four questions, 16–17, 95
France, *56,* 56

G

Gabon, 36–37
Good Friday, 5, 8, 34, 64, 80,
    81, 84, 91, 92, 100
Greece, 56
Grenada, 71
Guatemala, 71

H

Haft Seen, *23*, 23–24, *82*
hajl firuz, 43
Hanuman (monkey god), 28–29
Hasidic Jews, 94
Hayes, Rutherford B., 92
Hindus, 1, 25–30, 37, 41, 42,
    45, 65, 66. *See also* Holi
Holi, *25*, 25–29, *27*, *28*, *31*, *49*
    in Canada, 86–87
    festival of colors, 29, *28*
    in Fiji, 99–100
    in India, *41*, 44–45, *45*
    in Latin America and the
        Caribbean, *69*, 69–71, *70*
    in Mauritius, 25, 37, 86
    in Nepal, 25, 41, 42, 50
    in United States, *96*, 96
Holika, 25–26, 28, 42, 45, 50, 69
Holy Paschal, 46
home purification, 14
hot cross buns, 63–64, *64,* 65, 68, 98
Hungary, 57

I

Iceland, 57

imam, 43, 102
immigrants, 80, 81, 82–83, 85, 88, 91
indentured servants, 37, 66, 69, 102
India, 37, *41,* 42, *45,* 44–45, 66, 69
Inuit, 87–88, *88*
Iran, *76,* 76–77, *77*
Islam, 21, 32, 36, 43, 76, 102
Israel, 77–79
Israelite, 1, 11, 13, 16, 18, 95, 102

J

Jacob, 11
Jamaica, 68
Japan, 47
Jehovah's Witnesses, 82
Jesus Christ, 13, 20, 30, 42, 46, 50,
    52–61, 65, 68, 71, 84, 89, 92,
    99. *See also* Christianity
Jewish Children's Museum, *12*
Judaism. *See also* Passover
    Ashkenazi Jews, 17–18, 86
    Hasidic Jews, 94
    Jewish Children's Museum, *12*
    observant Jews, 14, 77, 102
    Reform, 95
    secular Jews, 16, 77, 103
    Sephardic Jews, 17–18

K

Kazakhstan, *42,* 46–47, *48*
Kiribati, 100
Kosher for Passover, 77–78
Krishna, 26, 28, 45
Kurds, *21,* 21, 102
Kyrgyzstan, 47–48

L

Latin America and the Caribbean,
    65, 65–74, *67, 69, 73, 74*
Latvia, *52*
Lent, 5, 7–9, 47
Liechenstein, 57
Lithuania, 57
liturgy, 38, 58, 102
lore, 28, 102

M

Malta, 58
Mardi Gras, 5
Maundy Thursday, 8, 34, 37

Mauritius, 25, 37, 86
Mayans, 72–74
Mediterranean, 4, 19
Mexico, 72–74, *73*, *74*
Middle East, 75–79, *75–78*
Moldova, 58
Mongolia, 48–49
monk, 64, 102
monotheism, 19, 32, 101
Moon, 4, 5, 6, 25, 48, 69
Moses, 11–13
Mwaka Kogwa, 39–40

N

Navruz, 19–24, *21*, 30, 42, 83.
    See also Mwaka Kogwa
    in Afghanistan, 43–44
    ancient traditions, 42
    in Canada, 87
    Haft Seen of, *23*, 23–24, *82*
    hajl firuz, 43
    in Iran, *76*, 76–77, *77*
    in Kazahstan, 47
    in Turkey, 51
    in Turkmenistan, 51
    in the United States, 97
neo-pagan rites, 1, 102
Nepal, 50
Netherlands, 58–59
New Zealand, 100
North America, *80*, 80–97, *81*,
    82, *84*, *88*, *90*, *92*, *93*, *96*

O

observant Jews, 14, 77, 102
Oceania, *98*, 98–100
Osterspende, 62

P

pagan traditions , 1, 3, 4, 52,
    55, 63, 64, 81, 102
Palm Sunday, 8
passion play, 65, 67, 73, 91, 100, 103
Passover, 6, 8, 11–18, *15*, *16*, *17*, 30
    in Argentina, 68
    in Canada, 86
    in Israel, 77–79
    in North America, *81*, 81–82, *93*
    in Russia, 60
    seder, 14–16, *15*, *16*
    in the United States, *92*, 93–96

Persian traditions, 2, 6, 19, 20, 22, 23, 24,
    39, 41, 43, 51, 75, 76, 82, 87, 97, 103
Philippines, *50*, 50–51
plague, 12–13, *17*, 18, 103
Poland, 59, *60*
Prahlada, 26–28, 30
prophet, 21, 44, 97, 103
Protestants, 6, 8, 9, 36, 39, 53,
    66, 80, 83, 88, 89, 100
Psalms, 15, 90, 103

R

Red Flower Festival, 43–44
Reform Judaism, 95
reincarnation, 27, 28, 103
Resch, Ronald, 84
Resurrection, 9, 46
Romania, 59
Russia, 7, 46, 53, 60
Russian Orthodox ecclesiastical
    calendar, 46

S

secular Jews, 16, 77, 103
Sephardic Jews, 17–18
Sham El Nessim, 34–35, *35*
shrine
    of Hazrat Ali, 44
    of saints, 22
Shunbun Hi, 46
Slovakia, 60
Slovenia, 60
South Africa, *32*, *38*, 38
Spain, 60–61, *61*
Sprinkling Day, 60
Suriname, *69*
Sweden, 61
Switzerland, 62

T

Tafsit, 33
Tonga, 100
Toonik Tyme, *88*
Tsagaan Tsar, 48–49
Turkey, 51
Turkmenistan, 51

U

Uganda, 39
Ukraine, *62*, 62–63

United Church of God, 81
United Kingdom, 63–64, *64*
United States, 88–97, *88, 90, 92, 93, 96*
Uruguay, 74

V

Vappu, 55
Vishnu, 25, 28

W

washing, of feet, 8
White House, *92*, 92–93

Z

Zanzibar, 39–40
Zion Christian Church, 38
Zoroastrianism, 19–21. *See also* Navruz

About the Author

Ann Morrill is a freelance writer, occasional bilingual editor, and adjunct college Spanish instructor living in Colorado. Her published writing includes poetry, opinion pieces, Spanish language phonics books, conservation articles, and creative non-fiction. She holds an M.A. in Latin American Studies from the University of New Mexico and a B.A. in history from Carleton College. When not writing or teaching, she enjoys hiking, reading, drinking coffee, and hanging out with her husband and two boys, Lucas and Marcos.